MW01234944

CULTUREShOCK!

SUCCESS

secrets to maximize

BUSINESS

in

BRITAIN

Peter North

Graphic Arts Center Publishing Company
Portland, Oregon

Photo credits:
Jerry Grandage: 22, 143
Mark Lim: 13, 18, 49, 53, 66, 97, 114, 182, 184, 187, 194, 197, 207, 210
Pat Munro: 23, 216
Peter North: 35, 58, 69, 95, 163, 171

This book is published by special arrangement with Times Editions Pte Ltd Times Centre, 1 New Industrial Road, Singapore 536196 International Standard Book Number 1-55868-481-6 Library of Congress Catalog Number 99-65080 Graphic Arts Center Publishing Company P.O. Box 10306 • Portland, Oregon 97210 • (503) 226-2402

Printed in Singapore

This book is for Pat and Don.

Contents

On Arrival in Britain

If you've heard all the reasons why you should avoid investing in Britain, the chances are you have been reading the British press or watching some programme on British television. When it comes to self-deprecation, the British are in a class of their own. The ability to be self-critical and take criticism from outsiders is one of the interesting traits of the British.

You read that the labour force is on strike, the sterling pound is dwindling to the point of oblivion (or alternatively rising to dangerous levels) and labour productivity is the worst in any first world country. Interest rates are high, the balance of payments deficit is widening and even more important, the English cricket team has just lost the second test match at Lords to a team of part timers from Zimbabwe, putting the home country at a score of zero to two for the series.

This sounds like a country in a permanent state of crisis. Bad news makes news. You scan the rest of the paper for a positive word and turn to the political pages for reassurance.

There you find that the House is closed for the summer recess and yet another cabinet minister has been discovered naked in a non-ministerial bedroom. Meanwhile, Prime Minister Tony Blair is still deciding whether or not to commit the country to full membership to the European Union (EU) and adopt the euro as the country's currency. Following a tradition of 20 years of dithering on the topic, he has decided to call on the Department of Trade and Industry to prepare another White Paper and defer a decision until the bureaucrats have had more time to upgrade the arguments for and against. After that, perhaps he will call a referendum a couple of years later.

Self-doubts are surfacing. Is this really a country you should invest in? Or should you merely transit at Heathrow and buy an onward ticket to Frankfurt?

But wait a bit. Your research department has listed all the advantages of setting up an operation in Britain. You scan through the list:

- Low taxes
- Absence of restrictive legislation
- No problems importing investment funds, repatriating profits or shifting currency about
- Sophisticated banking sector
- Ready-made market
- Access to EU markets
- English-speaking country
- Liberal investment assistance programme
- First class infrastructure
- Skilled workforce
- Reasonable labour rates
- Flexible labour markets
- The least regulated labour force in Europe
- Politically stable
- Sound macroeconomic policies

And above all,

- A highly developed enterprise culture

As the report says, this is a country that encourages overseas investment. A country that has been trading with the rest of the world for centuries. A country that in the past 20 years or so has become one of the world's freest economies. A country that is a centre of innovation and technical excellence.

As the report puts it, today's Britain is open for business.

Map of Britain

CHAPTER 1

Britain: Overview

Location

The British Isles are located on the western continental shelf of the European land mass. England, Wales and Scotland occupy the island of Great Britain, the largest island in the group. The other major island of the British Isles is Ireland, shared between Northern Ireland and the independent Republic of Ireland to the south.

Four countries, England, Wales, Scotland and Northern Ireland, make up the United Kingdom of Great Britain and Northern Ireland—a nation more commonly referred to as "Britain". Britain also includes a number of offshore islands, including the Hebrides, the Orkneys and the Shetlands.

The nearby British dependencies—the Isle of Man in the Irish Sea and the Channel Islands in the English Channel—enjoy administrative independence and are not considered part of Britain.

The commercial, financial and political heart of London lies along the banks of the Thames.

Since they legislate their own liberal income tax laws, both these regions are important to the financial sector. They support flourishing banking and investment industries.

British Origins

The majority of British people are descendants of a mixture of European races that invaded England in the first millennium. The original inhabitants of Britain, the ancient Britons, were Celts who were themselves the descendants of prehistoric European invaders. Later invaders established small settlements in various parts of the country. Even today, descendants of ancient cultural groups still maintain their original heritage. For example, people north of the Tyne in Newcastle are known as Geordies. Geordies are descendants of Germanic tribes of Danish extraction, who invaded the east coast in the seventh century A.D. and have stayed in the area ever since. In conversations among themselves, Geordies use expressions that may be incomprehensible to people in the rest of the country. In the same way, some Irish people can trace their lineage to the shipwrecked sailors of the 16th-century Spanish *Armada*, washed ashore on Ireland's rugged western coastline.

As descendants of various invading tribes who settled in different parts of the country, the British have never assumed a homogeneous nationality. There is no single British character type. Inter-tribal skirmishing, such as the perpetual problem in Northern Ireland, is still a daily feature of British life.

British in Business

British business culture is unpredictable. Some of your business dealings may be conducted according to rigid rules of protocol. Other dealings you may regard as extraordinarily unconventional. Britain is a highly individualistic society, where flair, originality and even eccentricity are valued traits. Some of the most successful people in British business have been unconventional characters, whose major claim to fame was their very unconventionality.

Old Chums, Friends and Family
The "old boys" of British public schools tend to maintain contact over long periods. Contacts made at school can be handy, even if it was a relative and not you that went to the school in the first place. A few years back, while working in a construction company, the author happened to meet the head of an engineering consulting company who had attended the same school as his father. This connection subsequently produced a number of construction contracts for the author's business.

The traditional view of business culture in Britain was of privilege rather than achievement. In this view, gentlemen would gather in clubs (from which gentlewomen would normally be excluded) and dabble in a board meeting or two, enjoy an extensive lunch culminating in port and cigars, then invite one or two distinguished associates home to their country mansions for fox hunting.

There is a grain of truth in this caricature, although it is less true now than 50 years ago—and it wasn't true even then. The class system in England, however, still turns out a steady stream of people of aristocratic bearing, who mingle easily with the rich and famous and find their way into business, usually in the "City"— a collective term for the financial services industry in London. In some cases, such people may be academically gifted. In other cases, their credentials may only consist of a good education and good contacts made at public school. The public school system still fosters the "born to rule" presumption that helped conquer the Empire in the 19th century. Armed with a cultured accent, their contacts and whatever academic qualifications they managed to achieve along the way, ex-public schoolboys set out if not to take over the world on behalf of the Crown, at least to carve their niche in the city of London.

As children of privilege, some ex-public schoolboys may launch straight into businesses they acquire through inheritance.

Virgin Atlantic

Richard Branson, founder of the *Virgin* brand that started its life on pop music record labels, is Britain's most prominent self-made man. The Virgin group has marketed its products using Richard Branson's personality as a marketing tool. One day Branson may be photographed in the Atlantic Ocean in a ditched hot air balloon (representing his attempt to be the first multimillionaire to circumnavigate the world utilising this specialised form of locomotion). The next day he may be handing over a cheque to an AIDS charity (funded by his company that sells "Mates" condoms). The day after he could be standing on the steps of a plane of his airline, Virgin Atlantic. One way or another, he is in the news almost constantly.

Branson likes to take on big business on its own turf and win. His particular *bête noire* in recent years has been British Airways (BA), which he accuses of running restrictive practices in the airline business, particularly over North Atlantic routes. Virgin Atlantic has succeeded both in court battles against BA and in operations on the intensively competitive North Atlantic market. A favoured Branson strategy is to target specific BA markets. In this vein, Virgin Atlantic has come up with a scheme to lease supersonic Concorde aircraft from Air France to compete with BA for those passengers bound from London to New York, who like to pay £2,500 for the privilege of flying across the Atlantic in half the normal time and at twice the regular speed.

Virgin has also obtained a franchise to operate rail services on the former British Rail system. Virgin is approaching the task of winning passengers to rail in its customary innovative manner. The company is introducing 40 high-speed tilt trains while having its section of the network upgraded.

Note: According to passenger surveys, while waiting for equipment and track upgrades to fulfil this dream, the company is having trouble running its conventional trains to published timetables. In a recent letter to a London daily, one user of Virgin's rail service suggested that Richard Branson should spend less time flying hot air balloons and more time in his office, getting his trains to run on time.

Or they may achieve commercial success by other routes, often through the City. A substantial number are eventually knighted for their services to commerce and finish their days in the House of Lords.

However, nothing prevents entrepreneurs from less privileged socioeconomic backgrounds from creating successful businesses in the private sector. For example, "Tiny" Rowland, the legendary CEO of Lonhro, one of the world's largest mining companies, received his education in a political internment camp in India—about as far from Eton as you can get. Rowland was at that time Rohlan, the son of German émigré parents detained during World War II.

The British admire eccentricity. Some British businesses have run extremely successful marketing campaigns around the quirks of their CEOs. Richard Branson is one of the most recognised faces of British business. Photogenic and charismatic, his highly unconventional business persona contrasts, for example, with the stereotypical Japanese business person whose dark blue suit blends in with his peers'.

The British People

Britain has one of the world's highest national population densities, at 240 people per square kilometre. The population expanded rapidly during the Victorian era, when families of 10 or 12 children were common. Since then, the rate of population increase has declined for many years. Like many first world countries at the end of the 20th century, the population of Britain has stabilised.

In 1997, the population increase was 0.27%. Fifty-five percent of this increase was due to net migration, with the balance due to a small surplus of births over deaths. According to the 1997 census, the population of the country was 57.6 million. By the end of 1998, Britain's birth rate had fallen to its lowest level—at 1.7 children per family. Demographers predict that the population of

Britain will continue to rise very gradually until about 2025, when it will peak before gradually declining.

History of Settlement

British settlement dates back to the Stone Age. Modern Welsh and Scottish people and their languages retain Celtic influences from that period. As the centuries unfolded, Romans, Danes, Norwegians, Saxons, Normans and others invaded Britain's southern and eastern coasts. Some invaders came to plunder and return home with the spoils of war. Others came to settle. For nearly a thousand years after the Normans took over in 1066 A.D., no invaders landed on British shores.

In the 1950s and 1960s, a new immigrant stream started to arrive from former British colonies, such as the West Indies, the Indian subcontinent and West African countries. Sufficient

One of Europe's most famous prehistoric monuments, Stonehenge was constructed over 5,000 years ago. The origins of Stonehenge and the purpose for its massive construction remain a mystery. Every year, millions of tourists visit the site, lured by the mystery and beauty that surrounds the stones and its environs.

> **The Millionaire Immigrants**
> Coming from a background in trading, Indians tend to be particularly active in retail, wholesale, and export and import activities in which they are often startlingly successful. By 1981, a survey to identify the rich and famous in Britain found that the most common surname for millionaires was the Indian name, Patel.

numbers of immigrants came to worry some in the predominantly Anglo-Saxon community.

Some national leaders in that era considered that assimilation of the new arrivals would be difficult. Political activists, such as Ulster politician Dr Enoch Powell, believed that the floodgates of immigration once opened might never be closed and warned of "rivers of blood" in a famous 1968 speech on racial disharmony. The majority of government members believed him and immigration from former British colonies was curtailed in the 1970s.

Then the African and Asian communities were concentrated in inner city areas where unemployment was high. By most economic indicators today, these immigrant communities are still racially disadvantaged, although the situation is gradually improving.

The Race Relations Act (1976) is the principal piece of legislation dealing with racial issues. Modern Britain is a reasonably harmonious society of mixed races, with little interracial conflict. Office of National Statistics figures for 1991 on ethnicity found that 94.5% of the population was "white", with the balance split between various African, Middle Eastern, Indian and Asian groups. Perceived difference in class rather than race was the main barrier separating people in everyday life.

Language
The official language of Britain is English. Because the English language has now become the lingua franca of the world, the

majority of the population does not bother to learn another language. Britain is essentially a monolingual country. Despite the increasingly close ties to Europe, the British government does not rate foreign-language skills as highly as other European countries. Whereas schools in continental Europe offer a minimum of two other European languages, the British government is deliberating over a proposition that its schools must offer a single European language alternative to English.

For a country that has not been invaded for one thousand years, Britain has preserved extraordinarily diverse regional cultures, which have produced a wide range of English accents and local dialects. Accents may vary from one town to the next—even between regions within towns. Accents may also vary greatly with social background.

The rural dialects of England, particularly western England, may be difficult for someone across the country to understand. Accents in the north of England are just as diverse. The Geordie accent of Newcastle is different from the Birmingham accent, which in turn, is different from the Liverpool accent, made famous in the 1960s and 1970s by The Beatles and other Liverpudlian pop groups.

Across the Irish Sea, the pleasant Northern Ireland brogue is reasonably easy to understand. Scottish accents, however, may well be incomprehensible to outsiders, particularly as many Scots employ their own specialised vocabulary, using words drawn freely from Gaelic.

Similarly, the Welsh mix English with words drawn from their own tongue. The Welsh are famous for their singing and their

A quiet village in Wales, where the people still converse in Welsh. An interesting fact about the Welsh and their language is that Wales has the longest place name in the world, containing 58 letters—Llanfairpwllgwyngyllgogerychwyrndrobwllllantysiliogogogoch!

accent has a delightful melodic lilt. Still an official language in Britain, Welsh traces its origins to the ancient Britons of the Stone Age. In the 1997 census, 26% of Welsh people claimed fluency in the Welsh language and 6% of Scots claimed fluency in Gaelic.

Early Days

In the first millennium, England alternated between being a kingdom and a collection of feuding fiefdoms. Which regime prevailed depended largely on the strength of personality of the monarch. For example, the territories of Great Britain that Edward I united at the end of the Middle Ages fell apart under the reign of his dissolute son Edward II. The balance of power between the monarch and other political stakeholders in the community was eventually settled in favour of the Parliament.

England and Wales have existed as a single political entity since the Middle Ages. Scotland was only absorbed into the federation after 500 years of border skirmishes The Scottish and English crowns were finally amalgamated in 1707, under the Parliamentary Act of Union.

It took another century to absorb Ireland. In 1801, the administration of Ireland transferred to London and the term *United Kingdom* was coined to cover the union of the four countries—England, Wales, Scotland and Ireland.

The Irish amalgamation was never a happy arrangement. The English had harshly conquered Ireland and the majority Catholic population was economically disadvantaged compared to the Irish Protestant minority. In 1922, by mutual consent of the British Parliament and the Sinn Fein—the dissenting Irish political party—the southern part of Ireland separated from Britain and became an independent nation. The six counties of Protestant-dominated Ulster, however, elected to remain in the union—an action that

Robert the Bruce and William Wallace were key figures in resisting invading English forces in the 13th and 14th century. Today, together with uniformed guards, their statues guard the entrance of Edinburgh Castle.

23

Old Scores

Inter-tribal conflict occasionally erupts amongst the tribes of Britain. Tribal hostility is most public in Northern Ireland, where the British army has maintained a peacekeeping presence since 1969. At issue is the perpetual conflict between Irish Catholics and Irish Protestants over their respective rights to Irish soil. This unresolved dispute stretches back many hundreds of years. Annual parades of the "Orangemen"—Protestants celebrating the victory of William of Orange over the forces of James II at the Battle of the Boyne in 1690—provide a catalyst for recurring bouts of inter-denominational conflict. To inflame the tension, Orangemen insist on routing their marches through Catholic districts. Green-clad Catholics respond with provocative marching of their own.

Elsewhere in Britain, ancient scores have been settled but not entirely forgotten. Scots, in particular, recount military operations fought by ancestors many centuries ago as if they had personally fought in them a few weeks before. The Battle of Bannockburn—a victory in 1314 A.D. of the Scottish highlanders over the invading English army—is a major annual commemoration in Scotland.

Likewise, ancient enmity between the English and the Welsh are alive and well in some parts of Wales, particularly in the north. A sign daubed on a bridge on the main road between England and Wales—"Free Wales from the English"—captures this sentiment. Some years ago, when the author was doing a project in North Wales, our English language signs were torn down and defaced on the grounds that they should have been bilingual, in English and Welsh.

produced the boundaries of the present United Kingdom of Great Britain and Northern Ireland.

A Brief Economic History

Seventeenth-century England had a rural-based domestic economy with little industry. By that time, England had virtually cut down all its trees and had switched from firewood to coal as a domestic fuel. Coal mining provided the impetus for the Industrial Revolution that swept first England, then the world.

During this period, mining coal and hauling it to the surface was an arduous and unpleasant business requiring virtual slave labour working under conditions of unbelievable hardship and brutality. Since mining was conducted below the water table, seepage into the mine had to be pumped out and discharged to surface streams. Steam engines were initially developed to drive the dewatering pumps of coal mines. They later provided the means to power the future machines of the Industrial Revolution.

The coal industry also provided the stimulus to develop transportation equipment and infrastructure to move coal from the mines to customers—first the canals, later the railways and later still, the steamships.

Once the Industrial Revolution got under way, technical innovators of the 18th century spawned a seemingly endless range of products and equipment. As the world's first industrialised economy, 19th-century England became "the workshop of the world", importing raw materials and exporting manufactured goods.

Britain lost its competitive edge, however, when other countries industrialised, particularly the United States and Germany. At the turn of the 20th century, Britain's predominant position in manufacturing was in decline. Britain's industrial infrastructure was older than competitor nations and therefore less efficient. The core industry by this time was steel making, since steel was the basic material of the Industrial Revolution. British steel making practice was outdated by better technology developed in Germany and the United States. Technological development— the cultural ethos of the Industrial Revolution—was no longer the exclusive preserve of Britain.

Today, the relative importance of manufacturing in the British economy has diminished. Service industries (such as banking, insurance, tourism and retail) have gained in strength to a point

Britain – A Statistical Overview (1997)

Population	58 million
Land Area	241,752 sq km
Capital City	London
Major Cities	Birmingham, Manchester, Cardiff, Glasgow, Edinburgh, Belfast
Official Language	English
Literacy	99%
Life Expectancy	Males 75 years, females 80 years
Population Growth Rate (1990s)	0.2% pa

Economy

Unemployment (1998)	5.7%
Inflation	2.8%
GDP	£756 billion (at constant 1995 prices)
Real GDP Growth Rate	3.7%
Currency	Pound sterling
Fiscal Year	Varies to suit the company. Tax year runs from 6 April to 5 April the following year.

Imports

Total Imports	£195 billion
Major Imports	Manufactured products
Major Import Sources	EU and North America

Exports

Total Exports	£177 billion
Major Exports	Manufactured products
Major Export Destinations	EU and North America

where they constitute the dominant sector in the economy. The manufacturing sector, however, is still significant, particularly in the export account. Manufactured products account for over 70% of British exports.

In the last two decades, the British government has adopted policies to modernise the country's infrastructure and industry and change the culture of enterprise. While most Britons consider these policies to have been successful, changes have not been achieved without some social cost.

British Trade

From the England of Sir Francis Drake in the late 16th century through to the present, Britain has been the dominant European naval power. As long as "Britannia ruled the waves", the island country was safe from invaders and free to pursue its global trading interests. Over the years, Royal Navy ships roamed the seas freely.

The Royal Navy gave British merchant ships the freedom of the seas and a secure diplomatic lifeline home. Trade, gunboat diplomacy and easy communication with the foreign office underpinned the rapidly expanding Empire.

Trade links developed between the home country and its colonies. The infamous "triangular" slave trade was established. Slaves were taken from the west coast of Africa, deposited in the

---

Mutiny on the Bounty

In 1789, a famous incident occurred that has been the subject of three movies and many books. Mutineers took over the Royal Navy ship, the *Bounty*. Such was the Royal Navy's fearsome reputation, the mutineers considered nowhere was beyond the navy's reach. The mutineers found a remote place, Pitcairn Island, on which to hide and burned the *Bounty* to conceal the vital evidence from a navy they were convinced would one day pay them a visit, wherever they chose to hide.

West Indies, where cargoes of sugar and spices were loaded aboard, and shipped to England. The third side of the triangle was the return to Africa with beads and trinkets—the currency used to purchase slaves from slave traders.

By the middle of the 18th century, the British claimed as its own about one-quarter of the planet's inhabited land area—geographically the largest empire any country had assembled since the dawn of history. The Empire's effortless expansion was based on trade rather than conquest. The British of the 18th and 19th centuries produced a number of extraordinary individuals, who brought vast tracts of land into the British sphere of influence by doing commercial deals with leaders of lands they annexed on behalf of the Crown. Almost singlehandedly, Cecil Rhodes acquired Rhodesia (which he immodestly named after himself), a nation that was five times the size of the home country. The acquisition of an entire country to be used for his own purposes made Cecil Rhodes an extremely wealthy man. This was a far more economical approach to empire building than the more traditional methods practised by some of Britain's European rivals in the great global carve-up of the 19th century—that of sending in expensive armies of occupation to ill treat and generally alienate the conquered subjects.

The British Empire reached its peak in the mid-Victorian age. After that, British influence diminished as each of the former British

Triangular Trade Revisited
A British tourist in West Africa recently observed a reversal of the triangular trade. On safari in the bush of east Gambia, locals selling beads and trinkets for US dollar bills assailed the tourist bus. "Only two hundred years ago," the tourist remarked, referring to the triangular trade, "we would trade our beads for their gold. Now we are returning the favour—trading our gold for their beads."

colonies obtained their independence, including India—the jewel in the Empire's crown—that became independent in 1947.

The Rise and Fall of Trade Unions

A number of factors reduced Britain's industrial competitiveness at the turn of the 20th century. None received greater publicity than the growth of trade unionism.

Britain was the birthplace of the labour movement. Unionism had its origins in the craft guilds of medieval times. But the advent of the Industrial Revolution revolutionised work practices and de-skilled much of the workplace. The manufacturing industry relied less on the skilled craftsmen of the previous era than on process workers tending the ever-expanding number of machines. Factories full of machines superseded cottages as the place of work.

The communist manifesto of Marx and Engels was written in Britain at the end of the 19th century. At the time, pay and working conditions in factories were appalling. After a century of exploitation, the British working class united to seek and improve their lot. The seeds of modern day trade union movement were sown.

The union movement grew rapidly. By 1892, 11% of the workforce belonged to a trade union. By 1920, the figure had risen

---

Maintenance on the London Underground, 1960s Style
Electricity to power signalling devices on the London Underground was run through cables on cable trays supported from brackets screwed into internal walls of tunnels and stations. Drilling the hole in the station wall for the screw securing the cable tray support brackets required three men from three different unions to operate a single power drill. The first layer of the wall, which was timber, required a carpenter. The second layer of wall, which was steel, required a fitter. The third layer of wall, which was concrete, required a mason. The maintenance gang was thus larger by at least two people than it should have been.

---

to 40%. Workers were no longer powerless—they took on companies, whole industries or in the case of the General Strike of 1926, the entire country.

No country developed trade unionism more trenchantly than Britain. The reputation of the British workforce for recalcitrance and truculence was widely reported. Perceptions of poor quality abounded. Industries, such as the car industry, developed an international reputation for quality problems, lack of productivity and late delivery. Labour issues were termed the "British disease" by competitor countries and Britain's European neighbours lived in fear of catching the "British disease" themselves.

In some respects, reports of British industrial disruption were exaggerated. In the 1970s, Britain lost fewer man hours per worker than Italy, Canada and the United States. But raw statistics do not tell the whole story. In the United States, unions tend to pick out a major company in an industry, such as General Motors, and put them out of business for months at a time, thus posting an impressive number of man-days lost. But when labour negotiations are complete and a new contract is signed, everyone returns to work for at least a couple of years.

British labour problems were more debilitating. British disputation tended to be localised as small-scale demarcation disputes, where unions would squabble amongst themselves about which of their members could do certain tasks.

A watershed event in British industry occurred in 1979. The British people voted out the Labour government of Denis Callaghan and voted in the Conservatives. Britain's first female prime minister, Margaret Thatcher, came to power during a period of unprecedented industrial unrest—the 1978 "winter of discontent"—when industry, government and the labour movement seemed in perpetual conflict.

The Thatcher government made one of the most radical economic shifts of modern times, stripping down the welfare state

> ## Labour Trouble and Strife: An International Comparison
> Contrary to some widely held beliefs, the workforce of modern Britain is less prone to disputation than competing countries. In 1995, working days lost to labour disputes per 1,000 workers in various countries were as follows:
>
> | | |
> |---|---|
> | Britain | 19 |
> | United States | 50 |
> | Australia | 80 |
> | Netherlands | 119 |
> | Canada | 130 |
> | France | 302 |

economy and replacing it with free enterprise. In doing so, it has entirely changed the work culture of Britain.

Legislation reduced the power of unions in various ways—exposing unions to lawsuits, outlawing secondary boycotts and mandating that strikes be decided by secret ballot (rather than a show of hands at a union meeting).

The government's battle with the union movement rumbled along for a few years and came to a head in the coal miner's protracted strike of 1984, which threatened to paralyse the country by withholding fuel supplies from the country's predominantly coal fired electricity generation system. The government retaliated by measures, such as importing coal. The issue became a stand off with neither side willing to budge. The Miners' Union was not successful in shutting down power supplies. Gradually, public opinion hardened against the miners. After an extraordinarily bitter industrial conflict lasting over a year, the miners were forced to capitulate. This was a turning point for industrial relations in Britain. The power of the labour unions was broken and unionism has been a diminishing force ever since.

Virtually all OECD[1] (Organisation of Economic Co-operation and Development) statistics relating to labour confirm a vast reduction of trade union activity over the last 20 years. By 1997, the union membership fell to below 28% of the workforce—down from its all time high of 49% in 1975. The number of working days lost through strikes was 250,000, lower than any other year on record. (For comparison, the number of days lost to strike in the "winter of discontent" of 1979 was 29 million, and in 1984, during the coal miners' strike, it was 27 million.)

The European Union (EU)

In 1958, six countries signed the Treaty of Rome to form the European Economic Community (EEC)—later changed to the European Community (EC). The political association of the countries in the community is now more widely called the European Union (EU).

The EU is an expanding organisation. By 1998, it contained 15 members: Austria, Belgium, Britain, Denmark, Germany, Greece, Spain, Finland, France, Ireland, Italy, Luxembourg, the Netherlands, Portugal and Sweden. Eleven other countries, mostly former communist countries from Eastern Europe, have also applied for membership.

The objective of the EU is to create a single economic trading community, including common rules of commerce, a single currency and a single European central monetary authority. In EU parlance, the process of achieving the integration of the economies of member states is called *harmonisation*. These goals were to be achieved in stages in accordance with various treaties, such as the Single European Act of 1985 and the Maastricht Treaty of 1992.

Subjugating the interests of member states to the overall objectives of the EU is taking some time to achieve. Cultural issues, such as patriotism and national pride, are at stake. Repugnant to some Britons, for example, is the proposed replacement of the pound sterling by the euro. Nonetheless, powers of individual member states have gradually been transferred to the European Parliament sitting in Brussels. The legal system has increasingly fallen under the jurisdiction of the European Court of Justice. The trend of transferring the powers of member states to EU administration is likely to continue.

Britain and the European Union

With its sphere of influence shrinking after World War II, British interest turned to Europe. On 1 January 1973, after a long and inconclusive debate with itself, Britain became a less than full-hearted member of the European Common Market (now the European Community). The decision to join Europe was far from unanimous. In the minds of many Britons of the early 1970s, the sun had yet to set on the British Empire. One effect of casting its lot with Europe was that Britain cut preferential trading ties with former colonies of the British Commonwealth.

British ambivalence towards financial and economic integration of Europe has not abated. While all the main political parties in Britain profess allegiance to the European Union, dissenting voices are heard across the political spectrum. Many British still fear a European hegemony dominated by the French and the Germans.

Under EU proposals the EU parliament will sit in Brussels, the EU Legal Commission will be in Luxembourg and the EU central bank in Frankfurt. London, the Euro-sceptics believe, may become a backwater. Others resent the fact that Britain's membership costs money—Britain is a net contributor to the EU budget (by about £2 billion pounds per annum).

Whether or not Britain has been economically advantaged in joining the EU has been notoriously difficult to prove.

However, the forces merging Europe are powerful and persistent. Despite the patriotic aspirations of citizens of member states, national powers are gradually transferring to the EU. In 1993, with the formation of the Single European Market, increasing numbers of pan European laws relating to trade and finance have been enacted. At the end of 1998, socialist governments were elected in Germany, France and Britain—three of the biggest economies in Europe—and the pace of European economic integration seems set to increase.

The move to harmonisation has attracted some criticism from the business community. Foreign investment conditions in Britain are perhaps the most attractive of any country in the EU. This could change as Europeanisation forces all EU countries to operate under identical laws. For example, harmonisation of corporate income tax may force Britain to raise its tax rate to the level of Germany's—thereby removing a competitive advantage of Britain as a destination for overseas investment. Harmonisation of employment conditions might impose additional obligations on employers—reducing the current flexibility of the labour market. Harmonisation of value-added tax (VAT) may require increasing taxes on currently exempt products.

Britain and the Euro

London has historically been the leading European centre for banking and finance and has so far maintained its position. There are, however, those who believe that with the financial integration of the European Union, this role may in the future be assumed by Frankfurt, Europe's future financial headquarters.

The European Monetary System (EMS) was set up in 1979 with the objective of achieving monetary stability in Europe by managing exchange rates within narrow limits. The European Exchange Rate Mechanism (ERM) was formed where the

---

The Euro

According to research by both Britain's largest unions and big companies, millions of jobs may be put at risk as a result of the decision to stay outside the European single currency. The research speculates that the main economic casualty of the decision will be a reduction of inward investment into Britain.

Euro notes and coins will start circulation on 1 January 2002. Existing European currencies will be withdrawn from circulation six months later, on 1 July 2002.

currencies of member states were denominated in European Currency Units, or ECUs. European currencies were only meant to move within "bands" having upper and lower limits. The idea was that when these pre-set limits were reached, central banks would enter the market to support or sell the currency as required by the situation.

History has proven the futility of efforts by many governments to regulate the value of their currencies over the long term. Limiting exchange rate movement through the ERM was no more successful than previous attempts by various central banks to fix exchange rates.

In 1992, currency speculators first attacked the pound sterling before turning their attention to the French franc. At the time, both currencies appeared overvalued. The leading speculator was George Soros, the New York-based Hungarian who a few years later, was blamed by Dr Mahathir of Malaysia for the downfall of the Malaysian ringgit in particular and the Asian economic implosion in general.

On 16 September 1992 (a date dramatically termed in the press as "Black Wednesday"), the speculators forced the sterling out of the ERM and the pound fell 20%. Repeating a familiar story of central banks around the world, the Bank of England lost about £4 billion of British taxpayers' money in a futile effort to keep the pound within the ERM band. Cashed up with their profits from the Bank of England, the speculators then moved across the Channel to attack the overvalued French franc. The results were similar. After the French franc succumbed, the ERM was pretty much abandoned. To accommodate the speculators, the trading "bands" of the currencies had to be expanded to plus or minus 15%—which was almost the same as having no bands at all.

At about the same time, the Maastricht Treaty of 1992 proposed adoption of a European common currency, the euro, for all member states. Being a single value for the whole of Europe, one advantage of the euro is that it would be harder for speculators to undermine than picking off weak currencies one after another as they did in Europe (1992) and in Asia (1997). The emotional downside is that individual countries in Europe would have to give up their own currencies. According to 1998 surveys, British public sentiment on the issue is 30% for the euro and 55% against (with the balance having "no opinion").

In the public mind, the principle objection to replacing the sterling with the euro seems to boil down to a simple non-economic issue. Many British are dismayed with the prospect of the face of the queen, now featured on all bank notes, being replaced by the 15 stars of "Euroland"[2]. More economically informed critics of the euro query how the monetary authorities can conduct an effective monetary policy using a single currency to regulate the economies of a disparate union of nations—some of which may be in recession at the same time as others are booming.

The incoming 1997 Labour government, sensitive as any of its predecessors to public opinion, decided to adopt a "wait and see" policy on the euro. A year later, Britain was still dithering about its commitment to the Maastricht Treaty to unify European currencies. It postponed the decision on whether to join Germany, France, Italy and eight other European powers in relinquishing their currencies in favour of the euro. For the time being, British currency is still the pound sterling.

Political pundits speculate that the Blair government will attempt to soften up British electors during the 1999–2000 period with a publicity programme in favour of the euro (to be termed a *familiarisation programme*)—to be followed by a referendum on the issue—tentatively pencilled in for late 2001. Meanwhile, commentators on both sides of politics express concern that Britain is staying on the sidelines while 11 of the 15 countries of the EU took the plunge into full euro convertibility on 1 January 1999.

Summary

Britain's long tradition as a trading and manufacturing nation continues today. Britain was the originator of industrialisation and experimented over most of the 20th century with a socialist economy. In the last two decades, the country has rediscovered capitalism in a big way. A new culture of entrepreneurialism, which initially required massive cultural adjustments to work. People lost their sense of holding permanent jobs.

While pockets of disadvantage remain, surveys measuring indices of community contentment generally found that the British feel better about themselves and their country than they did in the 1970s. The changes to a freer economy have been many. A major factor has been the policy of recent British governments to impose minimum restrictions on the movement of capital. Official British policy is to encourage inward investment. Another major advantage to Britain as an investment destination is the availability of a skilled and willing labour force to assist investors in attaining their investment objectives.

Chapter 2

Business Opportunities

General Business Environment

Overall, Britain has been good for business in the last few decades. In 1996, return on capital employed was 10.1%—the highest level for over 20 years. Unemployment levels are the lowest in the EU. Inflation has been contained. Investment levels are at an all-time high. Barriers to foreign companies are virtually non-existent. Quality of utilities is up to world standards and cost of utilities is lower than the EU average.

There are opportunities for both small and large businesses. Despite a record year in announced mergers between already large conglomerates, small business will most likely continue to play an important role in the British economy. There is no statistical evidence to support a popular view that the small business sector is disappearing. The indications are that the mix of small and large companies will continue in about the present proportions.

Small business received a significant boost under the privatisation policies of the Conservative government and this has continued under the Labour government, which returned to power at the 1997 election. Under the privatisation policies, the

---

The Government Line on Small Business

"Small businesses are the very embodiment of a free society—the mechanism by which the individual can turn his/her leadership and talents to the benefit of both the individual and the nation. The freer the society, the more small businesses there will be. And the more small businesses there are, the freer and more enterprising society is bound to be."

— Margaret Thatcher, 1989

Conservatives were keen to divest themselves of their business operations. To implement their policies, they subcontracted to small business many tasks that had previously been performed by direct labour.

Market Information

The Department of Trade and Industry (DTI) is the principal government organisation charged with encouraging and developing British industry. DTI operates through a number of subsidiary organisations throughout the country, which provide information, encouragement and financial assistance to existing industries and new companies. In addition, Britain offers a myriad of specialist government bodies, such as local tourist authorities dealing with particular industries in specific localities. (DTI offers an umbrella service that issues information on all forms of government assistance.)

The Gentle Art of Asking the Right Question

Marketing people take care to phrase their market research questions in a way that will get an honest response.

Surveyors into the pest treatment market, for instance, found it hard to get house-proud British housewives to admit to having cockroaches. Before they would do so, the British housewife had to be assured that everyone else had cockroaches too; whereas in France, the opposite occurred. French housewives were happy to chatter about cockroaches as soon as the subject was raised.*

Euphemisms may also cloud marketing issues. In a British survey into sanitary wear, a number of respondents failed to understand the question. "Of course we should encourage sanity in the bathroom", one of them replied.

* From *Marketing*, April 1997

DTI operates a specific unit, the Invest in Britain Bureau (IBB), to promote British commercial investment to overseas enterprise. IBB has branch offices in most countries in the world at which prospective investors can get advanced information on doing business in Britain.

In addition to DTI, many other private and public bodies can provide help and information. The Confederation of British Industry (CBI) is the private body that provides an overarching information service equivalent to DTI. CBI is the largest employer's organisation in Britain, with a membership of about 250,000 firms.

Other bodies that can provide information are the Association of British Chambers of Commerce (for most commercial activities and large and small businesses), the Federation of Small Businesses (representing small firms and the self-employed) and the Institute of Marketing.

The international market survey firm, A. C. Nielsen, collects comprehensive data for specific markets in the country. Statistical information is available from the National Office of Statistics at published prices, as reports on the Internet or on interactive CD-ROM.

At a local level, Britain has about 27,000 management consultants who can advise on the full range of business issues, including identifying potential markets and opportunities. Contact details and a snapshot of services offered can be obtained from the Management Consultancies Association.

Customer Feedback

A specific area of interest to DTI is "benchmarking", where companies obtain feedback from their own customers via a formal survey. Another is Competitiveness Achievement Plans (CAP), a formal scheme for companies to achieve industry best practice.

> **Unexpected Customer Feedback**
> Benchmarking assesses customers' feelings about their suppliers by written survey. Often the results of benchmarking surveys are a surprise. Companies that appear to be running smoothly and profitably can rate poorly in benchmarking surveys.
>
> In a 1998 benchmarking survey for Alfas Industries, a manufacturer of industrial sealants and poly-fillers with a turnover of £12 million per year, customers rated the company poorly in the key area of timely delivery of product. The executives of the company were amazed to learn of this problem and took immediate steps to rectify it.

Advertising

Advertising is a £12 billion per annum industry, with advertising revenues up 9% in 1996 compared to the previous year. There are about 2,000 advertising agencies in Britain, including well-known international names such as Saatchi and Saatchi, J. Walter Thompson and Ogilvy and Mather.

Advertising rules are free and easy. The Advertising Standards Authority (ASA) sets bounds of public decency and acceptability. Occasionally, advertisements violate guidelines of taste and honesty (particularly in regard to the disadvantages of a competitor's product) and have to be withdrawn. Restrictions are

Split of the Advertising Pound between Various Media (1996 Figures)

Media	Percentage of Total Expenditure
Press	54
Television	28
Direct Mail	12
Posters (including on transport)	3
Cinema	1
Radio	2

placed on the advertising of a small number of products that are perceived to have some antisocial aspects—for example, alcohol and cigarettes. Exceptions are made for sporting events, such as Formula One motor racing and cricket. Anti-smoking groups in Britain have lobbied to prevent cigarette companies from promoting the link between smoking and success in sport, so far without success.

One of the fastest growing sectors of the advertising industry in the 1990s has been the customer magazine market, where magazines are produced to highlight a particular product. The first customer-publishing magazine was *High Life* of British Airways, still going strong after it was established 25 years ago. The magazine successfully melded interesting stories vaguely related to the product with normal advertising copy. Companies marketing luxury products like BMW cars followed suit, as did companies providing a service, such as the Automobile Association. Now, companies marketing more mundane products, such as soap powder, dishcloths and chocolate bars, have hopped on the bandwagon, though their task to write riveting human interest stories on the virtues of the whitest whites or the most sparkling dishes present stern challenges to copy writers. Between 1990 and 1998, the output of the British customer magazine industry rose a staggering 314%.

The Importance of Shape

Tetly Tea bags was the second biggest brand name in its market, but market share was gradually falling to a combination of cheaper brand name competitors. Tetley investigated ways to arrest the decline of its product and came up with the idea of introducing the round tea bag (hitherto all tea bags had been square). After extensive market testing, the round tea bag was introduced and the product was successfully re-launched, securing its position in the market. As the only round tea bag in the market at that time, Tetley's market share immediately increased.

A typical farm in Britain. Wheat and barley are the main crops in Britain.

Agriculture

British agriculture is intensive, highly mechanised and efficient by European standards. It produces 60% of the county's food needs, with only about 2% of the country's labour force. Most farms are family holdings passed down from one generation to the next. The emerging trend in many countries to corporate farming has not been prevalent in Britain.

In recent years, British agriculture has been preoccupied by Mad Cow Disease. In 1996, Britain introduced cattle passports to control the travel of cattle between holdings. A total of 2.7 million British cattle were slaughtered before the disease could be eradicated.

The EU manages markets for agricultural products under the Common Agricultural Policy (CAP). The principal objective of this policy is to protect the agricultural producers of Europe by establishing floor prices for agricultural commodities. In practice, this has led to a seemingly permanent regime of tariffs on countries

EU Tariffs
Some tariffs the EU succeeds in levying on non-EU agricultural products are:

Canadian butter	300%
Japanese rice	550%
US powdered milk	179%
Frozen beef	215%

exporting to the EU from more efficient agricultural producers outside the EU. This may limit the access of food importers to British markets.

Producers outside the EU regard the CAP as protectionist. For this reason, it continues to earn trenchant criticism from agricultural producers, such as Australia and the United States, which face heavy tariff barriers exporting to the EU. Critics of CAP hold that the policy institutionalises inefficient EU farm practices, particularly in France, and is contrary to EU's general policies on liberalising global trade. These critics air their views on trade liberalisation at periodic conferences of the World Trade Organisation (WTO).

In 1992, the policy of the CAP shifted from stabilising prices to direct subsidies to EU farmers through various schemes. This led to additional criticism from within the EU itself since the policy appears to subsidise inefficient farm practices of some EU member countries, such as France, at the expense of British farmers, who are the most efficient agricultural producers in Europe

As Margaret Thatcher frequently pointed out in her tireless but unsuccessful attempts to reduce the British contributions to the EU, subsidising inefficient agricultural practices absorbs over 70% of the EU budget. Since Britain is an efficient agricultural producer, the CAP returns British farmers less in subsidies than the country contributes. According to Thatcher's argument, this arrangement penalises agricultural efficiency and perpetuates agricultural inefficiency. CAP policy continues to be reviewed, (with much resistance from vested interest groups). Reforms are produced at glacial speed. Altogether, the agricultural sector offers limited scope to the international investor.

Manufacturing

Bleak accounts of British manufacturing are reported in the British press with astonishing regularity. To paraphrase the words of Mark Twain, the death of the British manufacturing industry appears to have been greatly exaggerated.

What has happened in Britain has happened almost everywhere else. Manufacturing as a percentage of GDP has dropped. This is more a result of the rapid increase in the output of the service industries than an absolute decline in the

No-Skil Computer Systems

There are many computer driven production machines on the market spread across every industry. This is just one example.

In the field of CAD/CAM (computer aided design/computer aided manufacture) machine design, No-Skil Computer Systems is a name that says it all. The system, developed in Barnsley, Yorkshire, by the company Expert Control Systems, removes almost all the skill from the manufacture of a complex part. The computer programme to make the part is written automatically through a touch screen display using graphical and text prompts. No knowledge of programming is necessary. Once the programme is written for the particular part being made, the machine automatically controls its own tool paths, cutting speeds and material feeds. The machines will automatically sharpen tools that become blunt, and will continually check the dimensions of parts being produced, adjusting machine settings automatically to compensate for any wear of tools. Once the machine is set up, an almost limitless number of identical perfect parts can be produced with almost no human assistance. Technology such as this continues to eliminate jobs by replacing people with machines.

manufacturing industry itself. In fact, the output of British manufacturing has risen about 33% since 1980 and about 3% from 1990 to 1996. Over the same period, the manufacturing workforce has shrunk from 6.7 million to 4.2 million—reflecting dramatic rises in labour productivity from technological development, particularly in computer driven production equipment that requires almost no labour to operate. The labour statistics are often mistakenly reported as a decline in manufacturing rather than as a decline in manufacturing employment.

Output of Manufacturing in Britain

Sector	1996 production index*	1996 percent of total
Electrical and optical equipment	124.8	14.9
Chemicals	119.3	11.7
Oil and fuel refining	117.0	3.3
Rubber and plastics	113.3	4.9
Food and beverages	107.3	13.5
Tobacco products	106.9	0.8
Pulp and paper products	101.1	10.8
Transport equipment	95.5	10.6
Machinery and equipment	89.4	7.7
Wood and wood products	89.4	1.4
Textiles and leather products	89.2	5.1
Base metals and metal products	88.9	9.8
Other non-metallic mineral products	88.7	3.2
Other manufacturing	91.1	2.3
Total	100.0	100.0

*Based on 1990 index = 100

Note: The above is listed in order of rate of growth.

However, some pockets of the British manufacturing industry continue to experience problems, particularly the car industry. The industry for mass market and luxury British cars has now completely fallen into foreign hands—the German-owned BMW has taken over Rover Cars, Ford has taken over Jaguar and the German-owned Volkswagen has taken over Rolls Royce cars.

Ford and BMW have both run into production and marketing problems that receive continuing attention in the nation's press. Acres of British newsprint have been devoted to describing a labour productivity problem in Britain's biggest car assembly plant, the BMW Rover plant at Longbridge near Birmingham. The inference is drawn that such problems are endemic to the entire manufacturing sector. This is not true, even within the British car industry. By contrast to Longbridge, the purpose built greenfield Nissan plant at Sunderland, north-east England, has the highest labour productivity of any car assembly factory in Europe.

Manufacturing is spread all over Britain, especially in the Midlands and the north. It is a vitally important sector of the economy, and one much encouraged by the British government. At the end of 1998, the manufacturing sector accounted for 21.6% of GDP, 17.6% of total employment and 77% of exports. Segments of British manufacturing that are expanding the fastest are electronics, chemicals and food processing.

Britain is traditionally a manufacturing country with a skilled workforce and a highly-developed infrastructure. The country offers plenty of opportunities for foreign investors to get involved, including, in some cases, active government financial assistance.

Construction and Real Estate

The construction industry contributes about 5% to Britain's GDP. For domestic and commercial dwelling, construction building standards are in accordance with the Building Regulations issued by the Department of the Environment and administered by local authorities. Construction methods are changing. Across the construction industry, there has been a swing to off-site fabrication, with substantial sub-assemblies being brought to site for final on-site erection, rather than being entirely built on-site. Major construction companies therefore tend to have off-site assembly areas and many also have building products divisions.

Although the population of Britain has almost stabilised, the number of households rose from 16.5 million to 23.5 million between 1961 and 1995. The major part of this increase resulted from a reduction in average household size from 3.1 to 2.4 people per household. In 1997, the number of single-person households had risen to 28% of the total.

Recently, laws relating to the sale and purchase of property have been streamlined with the objectives of reducing the time required to complete the sale and obliging sellers to disclose more information regarding the property being sold. It is hoped that this will reduce the incidence of "gazumping", where the seller drops the original buyer to accept a better offer from someone else, and "gazundering", where the buyer threatens to withdraw from the sale unless the seller drops the price. Both practices have resulted in wildly fluctuating property prices in recent years.

Transportation Services

For both freight and passengers, road is the predominant mode of travel. Various government White Papers have studied ways and means of tempting people out of cars and onto public transport. Attempts to end the love affair between people and their cars have so far been conspicuously unsuccessful.

On a passenger mile basis in 1996, 86% of passenger travel within Britain was by car, 6% by bus or coach, 5% by train and 1% by air. Based on tonne-kilometres travelled, 81% of freight was by road, with most of the balance by rail. With much of the transport sector now privatised, opportunities regularly arise for new investors in the business of providing transportation services.

Britain's famous red double decker buses are often plastered with advertisements today.

Bus Services

A number of bus services were deregulated under the Transport Act of 1980. For the geographical areas in which it has been applied, the act has completely freed up the transportation system, leaving bus operators to set their own routes and timetables. A number of privately owned bus companies were formed in the 1980s. Some of them have been outstandingly successful.

British Rail

The privatisation of the former British Rail presents ongoing opportunities for private rail operators. The government's objectives in privatising the rail system were to reduce the losses made by the system and improve patronage. The government also has a social policy to promote rail travel in favour of road transport. Under this policy, the government is likely to continue to expand the system by progressively reopening railway stations which had

Stagecoach Plc

Stagecoach is perhaps the most widely known transport success stories in the country. In 1980, Brian Souter, a retired bus conductor with accounting qualifications and his sister Ann Gloag founded the company. The brother-and-sister team scraped together enough capital to purchase two second hand buses. In October 1980, Stagecoach made its first trip between Dundee in Scotland to London. The company's maiden voyage needed 25 passengers to break even. Thirty-five passengers showed up for the journey south, during which they were served snacks prepared by Cathy Souter, Brian Souter's mother.

From those small beginnings, Stagecoach grew quickly. It entered the market at the right time and was a major beneficiary of the programme to the 1980s to privatise almost all the bus services in Britain.

In 1992, Stagecoach expanded its transport vision when it became the first private company in 44 years to run a passenger service in Britain by including its own carriages on the London to Aberdeen overnight train. Years later, on the privatisation of British Rail, the company won the franchise to operate South-West Trains, the rail system in southern and western England.

By 1996, Stagecoach had become the largest independent bus operator in Europe, with operations in Africa and the Far East. Brian Souter was reputed to have become the wealthiest businessman in Scotland.

Note: Brian Souter has been a shameless self-publicist over his business career, with a particular penchant for appearing publicly in fancy dress. Like Richard Branson, he has conducted a marketing campaign for his company based on his eccentricities as an individual. His proud claim is that he has worn running shoes as business footwear during the entire time he was building his company.

previously been closed under the Beecham Plan of the 1960s for the rationalisation of railways.

Privatisation of the former British Rail has attracted its share of critics. What was once a single monolith has been split into more than 100 organisations, most private, some government.

Broadly speaking, under privatisation arrangements, privately-owned train operating companies (TOCS) lease rolling stock from privately owned rolling stock companies (ROSCOS) and run them on track owned and maintained by Railtrack, which was floated as a private corporation in 1996. TOCS are obliged to pay fixed charges to both Railtrack and ROSCOS for provision and maintenance of the track and the rolling stock.

Rail in Britain is not yet self-funding. Sixty percent of the revenue of TOCS comes from ticket sales, with the balance provided as a subsidy by the Rail Authority. The incentive to operators is that any increase of fare income they manage to achieve adds directly to the bottom line of the operation.

After about 10 years of operation, the re-organized rail system is still in its shakeout and bedding down period. Figures compiled by the government watchdog, the Office of Passenger Rail Franchising, show that the system is performing worse in some areas—in particular in train punctuality—than its nationalised predecessor, British Rail. Most of the problems the reorganised railway system faces stem from division of responsibilities. TOCS blame Railtrack for poorly maintained infrastructure. Railtrack blames TOCS for over-ambitious timetables. Under public pressure for improved performance, the Strategic Rail Authority is likely to strengthen regulations between itself and the various franchisees of the system.

TOCS franchise agreements are held for a fixed period and are then rebid. Franchises of the current operators expire in the year 2003, at which time business opportunities will open up for a new batch of operators to provide rail services to the public.

So far as other business opportunities in the transport area are concerned, the main transport assets that remained in public hands at the end of 1998 were the London Underground and the London Bus Corporation, both of which are likely candidates for future privatisation.

Minerals

The principal mineral mined in Britain is coal, with other significant minerals being gypsum, barytes, china clay and tin.

Coal was the main fuel of the nation for about 150 years. However, coal has a number of side effects that have made it less and less environmentally acceptable. Burning coal for home heating was banned at the end of the 1950s, with the objective of improving the air of cities, such as London, which was at the time regularly blanketed in smog. Coal also has a high sulphur content and puts a higher amount of greenhouse gas (carbon dioxide) into the atmosphere per unit of energy output compared to other fuels, such as natural gas. Coal is also expensive to mine.

The British Coal Board held a monopoly on coal mining operations in Britain until it was privatised in 1994. There are now no restrictions to the ownership of coal mining operations and anyone from the private sector, whether domestically or foreign owned, is entitled to participate, under the rules and regulations of the government and administered by the Coal Authority. Opportunities in the coal market are probably on the import side as uneconomic mines in Britain close down. There are no restrictions on coal imports or exports.

Oil and Gas

The oil and gas deposits of Britain are all offshore, lying under the UK Continental Shelf. The deposits belong to the Crown, but may be extracted under licence by private operators, whether domestically or foreign owned, under regulations issued by the Secretary of State. Most oil and gas extracted from offshore leases is landed in Britain. However, there is no statutory regulation that precludes operators from landing their products elsewhere. A petroleum revenue tax is levied by the Crown on hydrocarbons extracted from Crown leases.

Tourists arrive in droves every year to walk along historic Chester's beautifully-conserved streets. The medieval facades of Chester's famous shopping streets conceal unique covered promenades and retail shops.

Retail/Wholesale

Slighting its military traditions, the French general Napoleon Bonaparte once disparaged Britain as "a nation of shopkeepers". While exaggerated, the statement contains a kernel of truth. Retailing is certainly an area in which the British excel, from their exclusive shops to their mass-market outlets. As well as chains of shops within Britain, most of the large British retailers also have successful operations overseas.

About 300,000 retail and wholesale businesses do business in Britain, ranging from a large number of small shops to a small number of very large retail chains. The large chains have their own buying departments, whereas smaller shops belong to co-operatives that buy on their behalf—exerting sufficient purchasing power to keep the wholesale prices reasonable. With extended

> **Retail Efficiency—The Beneficiaries.**
>
> By most measures, retail in Britain is efficient. According to a 1998 report by management consultant McKinsey, the average British supermarket sells twice as much produce per unit floor area as comparative stores in the United States and Europe.
>
> Opinion is divided whether this efficient use of assets translates into better prices for consumers. According to a 1998 survey by Britain's biggest supermarket chain, Tesco, a survey of a basket of products by market researchers A. C. Neilson demonstrated that their stores had a price advantage over equivalent stores in Belgium and Italy. However, this claim was disputed after a survey by the British investigative newspaper, *The Sunday Times*, which claimed that the Neilson analysis had failed to account for the lower rate of VAT in Britain on most food items in the survey basket. The view of *The Sunday Times* was that the efficiencies of British retailing are being passed onto shareholders of supermarkets rather than customers.

shopping hours, one of the principle areas of competitive advantage of the corner shop has been removed. Most industry commentators expect that the industry will continue to consolidate over the years, with a trend to smaller numbers of larger shops.

The most successful supermarkets are large complexes at the edge of town, rather than town centres. The government is presently discouraging this practice, since the developments encroach on the countryside and encourage car use. For this reason planning permission for construction of new centres will be granted reluctantly, if at all. Instead the government's policy is to revitalise shopping in existing High Streets.

The major supermarket chains are continually installing labour saving devices to cut costs. A few years ago, Tesco went as far as to experiment with a couple of shops with no check-out staff at all. Subject only to random spot checks, the customers merely scanned in their purchases and booked their transactions to their credit cards. In such shops, it is claimed, one can perform the entire shopping routine without contact with another human being. Even in supermarket style shops that haven't quite reached this degree of computerisation, the current fad for cost cutting has rendered assistants fairly thin on the ground.

Retailing in Britain has been dominated by British firms, most of which are also active in overseas markets. However, in 1998, the US retail giant *Wal-Mart*, after a successful foray into the German market, announced its plans to establish a chain of supermarkets into Britain through judicious purchase of sites of failed British chain stores.

Internet Selling
A recent innovation in retail is Internet shopping which has been introduced on a trial basis by the larger supermarkets including Tesco and Sainsbury the number one and two British supermarket companies. Under this scheme, the consumer phones in and is taken for an interactive tour of the shopping aisles via a computer

Shopping on the Internet

For all the pizzazz generated by notions of Internet shopping, however, it's hard to beat the advantages of a supermarket where the customer provides the following services free of charge to the retailer:

- Stock picking (customers load their own shopping carts) and self serving (customers wheel their carts of goods to a central check-out point)
- Virtually no packaging of goods required (they go into a minimum cost plastic bag to be carried by the consumer)
- No delivery (the customer conveys the goods from the shop to the carpark, then to the point of use and performs all loading and unloading duties in and out of their own cars)

For Internet operations, the costs of goods handling and delivery may well exceed the costs of providing shops in the first place. So far this has been the experience of Internet bookseller, Amazon.com, when competing against more conventional booksellers. Despite massive sales, Amazon.com has failed to make a profit in its first years of operations due to the cost of stock handling.

monitor. The consumer punches in an order via the computer keyboard plus credit card details and the order is shipped.

If this becomes the preferred shopping method of the future, it will turn retailing on its head once again by reversing the present expansion of large shopping centres. Internet shopping theoretically requires no shops at all with the goods being supplied directly from warehouses.

Nevertheless the idea of Internet shopping has its adherents in the retail industry and sales over the Internet are growing rapidly. In 1998, 60% of British companies were using the Internet to buy and sell at least some of their raw materials or products—compared to less than 10% in 1997. The value of products bought through the net was £200 million in 1997 and £406 million in 1998. This figure is estimated to go to £6.14 billion in 2001.

There are some particular niche areas in the retail market where Internet shopping is particularly suited in Britain and elsewhere. For example, an extraordinarily difficult area to legislate is the trade of goods exploiting differences in laws between countries. Internet trade threatens to make national trade restrictions ever more meaningless and taxes, such as VAT, ever harder to collect. Items, such as software, any form of graphics, photography and anything that can be reduced to digital data and transferred electronically, can now be sent and received over the net. Doctors can diagnose the ailments of patients whom they will never meet because they live on the other side of the world. Architects can transmit building plans over phone lines. Authors can send books. Musician can send recordings. International sales of such intellectual property is virtually impossible to control and/ or tax. Britain, as one of the principal providers of software and high-tech services, is likely to be a beneficiary of this trend.

Financial Services
London is the most important centre in Europe for the provision of financial services, and along with New York and Tokyo, it is one of the three most important financial centres of the world. London has more banks than any other centre, the largest foreign

The Bank of England is the centre of Britain's financial sector.

> **Business in Britain—Too Good for Some?**
> In recent years, business conditions have been favourable in Britain. There have been few major bankruptcies or receiverships in recent years. One of the industries in Britain which has suffered as a result is the insolvency industry. An executive of the accounting firm KPMG (en route to Bangkok) was recently explaining his move to Thailand, where, in the wake of the Asian economic implosion of 1997, the insolvency business was booming (KPMG calls insolvency "corporate reconstruction"), while the opportunities in prosperous Britain were limited.

exchange market, and the largest market in the world for trading foreign equities. It ranks second for the size of its mutual funds industry and the size of its insurance market. Other large markets are commodities, derivatives trading, insurance bonds and general financial services. In addition to London, major centres in Britain for the provision of financial services are Manchester, Cardiff, Liverpool, Leeds and Glasgow.

Banking

Banking in Britain has been subject to only a modest degree of statutory control. The controlling legislation is the Bank Act of 1979 and amendments of subsequent years. The act provides that all banks and other institutions into which the public deposits money must be licensed by the Bank of England.

Foreign banks can operate in Britain provided they obtain the appropriate licenses. Use of the word *bank* in the name of an institution taking deposits is only allowed under fairly stringent Bank of England rules. Less stringent rules apply to the licensing of non-bank lending institutions, such as building societies. Banks must have a minimum capitalisation of £5 million. The equivalent figure for building society capitalisation is £1 million.

The Bank of England operates a deposit protection scheme whereby the security of customers' deposits is guaranteed. The banks must lodge a cash security equal to 0.5% of their liabilities with the Bank of England as premium for this scheme. Should the bank become insolvent the fund will reimburse a minimum of 75% of the funds of small depositors.

Commercial Banks

British retail banks have expanded their activities from a mere clearing bank role to a wide range of financial services such as raising capital, foreign exchange dealing, leasing, factoring, and providing financial advice. Bankers in Britain pride themselves on being able to oblige almost any requirement of their foreign clients. For those foreign investors who wish to remain with their domestic banks, most foreign banks also have branches in London. Britain probably has the least regulated banking industry of any major industrial country in Europe. Almost any conceivable transaction can be conducted. This almost carefree attitude can have its advantages, particularly from the viewpoint of a foreign investor. On the other hand, it can have its downside too.

The Barings Story

Easy regulation has its downside for depositors and on occasions, for the bank itself, as demonstrated by the 1994 collapse of the venerable bank Barings plc. Internal auditing of Barings was so inadequate that Nick Leeson, the bank's nefarious futures trader in Singapore, managed to exhaust his bank's entire global capital stock buying vast quantities of stock option futures on the falling Tokyo stock market. While SIMEX (the regulatory authority in Singapore) was aware of Barings' extended position, none of the executives in Barings' London office had the slightest inkling that Leeson was gambling away the entire capital of the bank until well after the event. After that, the bank lacked the resources to save itself. It was subsequently taken over by Dutch bank, ING.

For many years, the industry has been dominated by an oligopoly of established banking institutions—Barclays, National

Westminster, Lloyds, Midland—with an established infrastructure of branches. In the past, it has been difficult for new banks to gain a foothold in this market.

In an effort to reduce the costs of handling transactions, retail banks have been promoting electronic banking for some time. Consumer acceptance of electronic commerce is now higher than in most countries. People have been weaned away from cash and checking accounts and pay a high proportion of their accounts by direct debit.

This programme of cultural condition conducted by major banks to reduce transaction costs may ultimately act against them. With the advent of telephone and Internet banking, the many branches of the big banks currently dominating the retail banking industry may in the future become more of a high cost liability than an asset. Phone or Internet banking transactions cost a fraction of the same service over the counter.

New entrants have already emerged. One of the latest is Egg, the banking venture of Prudential Corporation into telephone banking in the retail market. Supermarket chains Tesco and Sainsbury have also floated banking ventures that at the end of 1998 had attracted about one million accounts. The retail banking industry in Britain offers the opportunity for new entrants in the financial services industry.

Building Societies

Building societies are regulated under the Building Societies Act of 1986. The original purpose of building societies was to provide finance for home building. Over the years, building societies have increased the range of financial services they offer, including current accounts and cheque guarantee cards. Under competition from building societies, banks have fought back by focusing on the home loan market. Since building societies operate in most banking markets, some economic commentators hold that British building societies are a logical takeover target for foreign banks wishing to enter the British banking industry.

Merchant Banks

The term *merchant banks* derived from banks established by the merchants of London to provide financial support to their main occupation of selling merchandise. Later, provision of the financial services themselves became a merchantable product and the now lucrative merchant banking industry became established in its own right as an industry providing financial services to the business sector. All the leading merchant banks of the world have their headquarters or a branch office in London.

Merchant banks may be useful to foreign investors in areas such as raising short-term debt funding, raising capital, obtaining financial advice, merging or joint venturing with local firms and takeover activities.

Merchant banking is particularly prominent in British business culture. Like the United States, British business of recent years

---

Takeovers and Mergers—Are They Good for You?

Whether takeovers or mergers are good for the general economy, or for some sections of the economy, is a subject of continuing debate amongst economists and other interested parties. Proponents of takeovers point out that takeovers free up capital to flow to where it can most productively be used. Opponents claim that feeling threatened by takeovers, management of target companies become obsessed by the short term, with next year's bottom line profit (which if high makes the target company harder to take over) being given more consideration than more worthy policy objectives like long term investment.

One thing everyone is agreed upon. Principal beneficiaries of the takeover boom are the company executives orchestrating the merger, the shareholders of target companies and the merchant banks advising both the target and predator companies.

has been driven more by short-term financial considerations than, for instance, the more long-term view taken by countries like Germany and Japan. Short term profit is pursued aggressively, with every company a potential target for takeover. The merchant banking industry, which makes a great deal of its income from takeover activity, fosters the view that a dynamic corporate structure is economically healthy.

There is no doubt that British merchant banks are Europe's leading exponents of mergers and takeovers, simply because more large mergers and takeovers occur in Britain than the whole of the rest of Western Europe put together. The number of contested takeovers handled by the City averages about 40 per year; in Germany, there have been less than half a dozen since the end of World War II. British banks have more experience in the field and there are more of them to compete for whatever merger and takeover business is available.

Money Market

Apart from bank accounts, money is lent and borrowed as short term assets and debts, such as bills of exchange, Treasury Bills or foreign currency denominated loans (termed "Eurodollars" or "eurocurrency" depending on the currency selected). London, New York and Tokyo are the three biggest markets in this business. Financial trading is mostly conducted by discount houses located within a small area (around Lombard Street) in the City.

London banks offer a full range of foreign exchange transactions—an industry reckoned to net an aggregate of £20 billion to £25 billion a year in transaction fees. This business is somewhat threatened by the move to the euro, the single European currency. Customers trading within Europe will no longer need to switch currencies as they move money around. Nor will dealers have the opportunity to profit from arbitrage positions they currently exploit on interest rate differentials between various currencies. In addition, the banking industry estimates that the mere act of converting their systems to accommodate the euro will cost over £1 billion. On the other hand, adoption of the euro may create new business opportunities in euro-denominated bonds and securitisation, with money flowing from Tokyo and New York, as the euro establishes itself as the preferred international currency. The net effect on the British banking industry of the switch to a single currency is unclear.

Insurance

London is the historical centre of the insurance industry. The notion of insurance was born in the late 17th century when shipowners gathered at the London coffee house of Edward Lloyd to discuss how they would protect their ships and their cargoes from bad weather, pirates and the sundry perils of the sea. These discussions gave rise to Lloyds of London—still the most famous name in the insurance business. In recent years, the news for Lloyds hasn't all been good, with massive losses incurred from events as diverse as terrorist activity, freak weather conditions and oil tanker disasters. Despite these setbacks, the name lives on. The proud claim of Lloyds is the ability to underwrite any risk. Other major insurance companies, too, have based their operations in London as the financial centre of Europe.

Tourism

Tourism contributed £38 billion to the economy in 1997, equivalent to about 5% of GDP. About 1.8 million people are employed in tourism and related industries. Money spent by overseas tourists visiting Britain in 1996 was £12.4 billion compared to £16.3 billion spent by British tourists overseas. Fifty seven percent of British holidaymakers spent their holidays in Britain. Of the balance, 70% spent their holidays elsewhere in Europe.

The most visited tourist attraction in Britain is the pier and associated beach front area in Blackpool in Lancashire on the Irish

Tourism is a major industry in Britain, accounting for about 5% of GDP. Besides increasing numbers of Asians and other Europeans, the British themselves choose to spend their vacations in Britain. Here, we see Asian and European tourists at the ruins of Coventry Cathedral.

Sea. The next most popular tourist destinations are the British Museum and the National Gallery, both in London.

The regional tourism industry offers opportunities for operators to receive financial assistance for groups interested in promoting tourism in their areas. The Wales Tourist Board and the Northern Ireland Tourist Board, for example, both operate schemes to subsidise the development of tourist infrastructure.

Health

The principal administrator of health services in Britain is the National Health Service (NHS), a government administrative body run by the Department of Health. During the early 1980s, the government became concerned that health costs were rising much faster than the GDP. Health costs of the old age group were much higher than the national average. Also identified was over-servicing by doctors, particularly in the area of prescription drugs. By imposing budgets on doctors, the government not only reduced NHS costs, but also reduced the profits of drug companies.

Commercial opportunities in the health sector are in the corporatisation of medicine. Traditionally, doctors and dentists set themselves up as cottage industries, either practising alone or sharing a practice with two or three others. With the increasing cost of state-of-the-art medical and dental equipment, plus the increased demands of the NHS bureaucracy, this approach becomes progressively less economic. Medical and dental practitioners are increasingly likely to work for large clinics owned by medical companies.

After a move by NHS to contract out almost every service, including their mainstream labour needs, labour hire companies in Britain have benefited from hiring medical staff to hospitals. The biggest commercial opportunities in healthcare are those outside the NHS system. Cosmetic medicine and dentistry has expanded enormously in recent years, a trend that looks likely to continue. Future opportunities in the private health sector look good.

Franchising

Franchising, a halfway house between owning a business and working for someone else, is a business arrangement that has been growing for two decades. Statistics quoted by the Franchise Association claim that businesses starting up as franchises are half as likely to fail as non-franchise businesses. The biggest name in British franchising is the US fast food chain, McDonald's.

Summary

The British government has been extremely business-friendly for a number of years and the sentiment seems likely to continue. While governments have had essentially laissez faire policies for the last 20 years, they do have an interactive industry policy aimed at encouraging investment in Britain, whether foreign or domestic. The principal organisation charged with the task of developing the private business sector is DTI. DTI operates offices under different names, such as the Invest in Britain Bureau, which perform various services to assist inward investors. Marketing information is easily obtainable both from the government and from the private sector. Britain is a natural home to many industries, among them manufacturing, financial services, insurance and tourism. Opportunities exist in the transportation and utilities areas due to the recent privatisation of these industries.

CHAPTER 3

Government, Inward Investment and Taxes

British Political History

Britain was the first modern country to develop the institution of political democracy. The so-called Westminster System has served as the model for most of the democracies that have emerged around the world over the past 200 years.

Britain remains a constitutional monarchy. Over the centuries, the institution of British monarchy has endured with diminishing power. Whereas past English kings governed the country from the throne, the monarch today reigns but does not rule. During the last 200 years, power has shifted from the monarchy to the democratically-elected government, reducing the monarch to a figurehead position.

The British Parliament sits in London, at the Houses of Parliament in Westminster, on the left bank of the River Thames. The Parliament consists of two bodies, the House of Commons, which is the main law making body, and the House of Lords, which is notionally a house of review.

The House of Commons consists of 659 members who represent constituencies in a "first past the post" system. Parliamentary elections for the Commons must be held at least once every five years but can be called earlier at the option of the ruling party.

The House of Lords, an upper house with limited powers of review but no power to veto legislation, has a mixture of hereditary positions and members who are appointed for the duration of their lifetime—usually as a reward for performing some sterling task for the community during their working lives. Margaret Thatcher

The Houses of Parliament and St. Stephen's Tower on the right—better known as Big Ben, the name of the bell within it—were built in the 19th century along the River Thames.

is a member of the House of Lords, as is Sir Roy Jenkins, a previous Labour government chancellor of the exchequer. Cynics hold that one of the major purposes of the House of Lords is as a repository for politicians who have passed their use in the Commons. As Claus von Bulow pointed out in a satirical reference to the political stability of Britain, Stalin once had to shoot some generals because he didn't have a House of Lords to put them in.

Over the years, the House of Commons has succeeded in acquiring power from both the monarchy and the House of Lords. Today, the monarchy is merely an institution used to perform ceremonial roles and the House of Lords is almost irrelevant other than as the final court of judicial appeal.

British Political Parties

During most of the 20th century, two major political parties have dominated British politics. The Conservative party, originally a party formed by disaffected Irish peasants, has changed completely over the years and is now the respectable political face of business and landed interests. The Conservatives are often called *Tories*, which was a 19th century political party not related to the present day Conservatives. The other major political party of the modern era is the Labour party, which originated from the Labour movement of the early 1900s.

Since World War II, elections have been a contest for middle ground that both major parties seek to occupy. As in many democracies, the ideology of major parties can be difficult to distinguish as each party seeks to present policies they think will appeal to the average voter. The background of candidates for election from both sides of politics has approached the centre. When selecting their candidates, the Conservatives have shed aristocrats at about the same rate that the Labour party has shed ex-blue collar workers. Over the past few elections, both parties have almost succeeded in making themselves philosophically indistinguishable. As a result, come election time, personalities of the party leader and perhaps some senior colleagues have, more than other factors, determined the outcome of recent elections. People vote for the party whose leaders they like the most. Or if they are sceptics, they may vote for the leaders they dislike the least.

As well as the Labour and the Conservatives, minority parties in Britain win seats in the Parliament and occasionally hold the balance of power. Some minority parties present alternative national policies. Others push regional issues. The Liberal Democrats, a party having its origins in the 19th century, has consistently managed to win seats in the 20th century. Regional parties winning sufficient votes to send their candidates to the current Parliament are the Ulster Nationalists, the Welsh party (who call themselves by their Welsh name—Plaid Cymru) and the Scottish Nationalists.

Changing Political Sentiment

Political sentiment in Britain and much of Europe swung to the right during most of the 1980s. Right-wing governments held power in Britain, France and Germany. The communist bloc of eastern Europe failed during the period. The decade saw a massive sell off across Europe (and the world) of government assets into private hands. Britain, under Prime Minister Margaret Thatcher, was a pacesetter in privatising public assets.

The Conservatives replaced Margaret Thatcher as leader in 1990 with John Major. Thatcher resigned from the House of Commons shortly afterwards. She was later awarded the title Dame Margaret and appointed a Life Peer to the House of Lords.

Under John Major, the Conservatives succeeded in winning the 1992 election but with a reduced majority. By 1995, however, the government had been in power for nearly 20 years and the favours and sinecures it had granted over the years to outgoing

---

Parliamentary Favours

In 1994, a scandal was uncovered in the Parliament—members were being paid by private companies to ask questions in the House that would advance the companies' interests. Initially, two backbench Ministers of Parliament (MPs), David Tredinnick and Graham Riddick, were implicated in this practice. Later, allegations were levelled against two ministers, Tim Smith and Neil Hamilton, that they had used their positions in the House to advance private causes. Both ministers were forced to resign

In another typical scandal of the era, Conservative backbencher Keith Best was forced to resign after it was found he had used false names to apply for increased quantities of British Telecom shares when that institution was privatised. Having left Parliament in disgrace, the Conservative party rewarded Best with a sinecure position as director of a government quango (quasi autonomous government organisation)—the Immigrants Appeal Panel.

politicians and favoured members of the business community were starting to become an electoral burden.

Before the 1997 election, pollsters realised that Britain, along with much of Europe, was experiencing a swing in public opinion. Having dabbled in the right for a decade, electors were returning to their customary position—centre—or in this case, just left of centre. In Britain, the "sleaze factor" that Labour managed to pin onto the hapless Conservatives merely reinforced this shift in sentiment.

1997 General Election

In 1997, Tony Blair's Labour party swept to power in Britain, putting to an end 18 years of Conservative rule that spanned four elections. Blair projected an image of youth and vitality to contrast with the stolid—some would say boring—style of the outgoing Conservative leader, John Major.

As the election neared, the Conservative government looked tired. Electors voted in overwhelming numbers for a change.

Composition of the House of Commons (May 1997)
Members returned to the House of Commons after the 1997 elections were from the following parties:

Labour	419
Conservative	165
Liberal Democrats	46
Ulster Unionists	10
Scottish Nationalists	6
Plaid Cymru (Party of Wales)	4
Social Democrats	3
Sinn Fein (Irish)	2
Democratic Unionist	2
UK Unionists	1
Independent	1
Total	659

Immediately after the election, John Major, the outgoing prime minister, headed to Lords Cricket Ground to watch the most English of games—declaring to the world his future disinterest in politics.

Proposals for Political Reform

There are fewer political checks and balances in the British political system than most democracies. The system is simple. The party that wins a majority in the House of Commons controls Britain. Within the Commons itself, power is exercised by a small clique of ministers, headed by the prime minister. The balance of the government's majority—the backbenchers—will almost always vote along party lines. Party members who fall out of favour can quietly retire and be given public administration positions. By the end of 1996, after 18 years of Conservative rule, about 7,700 new quangos had been set up, into which ex-parliamentarians could be put out to pasture.

The almost unfettered power of the Commons and thereby of the Cabinet concerns critics of the British political system. Political commentators point to other democracies in Europe and elsewhere, where the houses of review enjoy the power to balance the prime minister and his Cabinet. Germany has its Bundestat. France has its Senate. In the United States, the president has to obtain approval for most measures from both the Congress and the Senate.

The proposition to curb the power of the Commons must be voted on by the Commons before it can go to referendum and thereafter become law. History shows that while the opposition in the Commons usually thinks a house of review with real power is a good idea, once the opposition party gets into government, the sentiment changes.

The House of Lords—the Notional House of Review

Four types of Lords are entitled to sit in the House:

- Hereditary peers (756 members)
- Life peers (738 members)
- Lords of appeal (24 members)—judges of the highest court of appeal.
- Spiritual: archbishops and bishops (24 members)

A seat in the House is a birthright of hereditary peers. Other Lords are appointed, either for the term of their natural life, or until some stipulated retirement age.

The House of Lords has only limited power of review. It cannot delay a money bill longer than a month. Other bills held up in the Lords and sent back to the Commons will come into law within one year of the second reading in the Commons, even if the Lords fail to pass them a second time. The main function of the House is to act as the final court of appeal for the judicial system.

Reflecting its status as a moribund institution that has passed its use by date, the House of Lords has developed a reputation more as a gentlemen's club for landed aristocrats and retired politicians than an institution of serious political debate. Discipline in the House is lax and absenteeism is rife. The number of seats in the Lords is 1,542, with an average attendance over the past decade of 320, of whom, according to critics of the political process, about half are likely to be asleep at any one time. The average age in 1998 for members of the House of Lords was 74.

Agitators for political change have noted that perhaps the country is getting out of the House of Lords merely what it pays for. Other than travelling allowances for trips between the House and their country estates, the Lords draw no salaries for their contribution to governing the country.

The queen's speech for the opening of Parliament after the 1998 summer recess announced that a bill would be introduced "to remove the right of hereditary peers to sit and vote in the House of Lords". Despite cries of "Shame!" from a few ermine clad figures in the chamber, the bill is likely to be passed into law.

The Case for Proportional Representation

Also under active debate is the "first past the post" voting system. Virtually all other European countries have some element of proportional representation in their systems for determining the outcome of elections. The underlying idea behind proportional representation is to allow parties to obtain seats in government based on the number of votes cast for each party. The system allows smaller parties to get people into Parliament more easily than the "first past the post" system operating in Britain.

Proportional Representation—For and Against

Critics of proportional representation point out that the system can thwart the ideals of the democratic process. Under proportional representation, parties with a tiny proportion of votes can, and often do, hold the balance of power. Thus in postwar Germany, no government has held office without the support of the tiny Free Democrat party, which has called the shots in Germany in four decades despite attracting less than 10% of votes. Similarly, in Sweden, to stay in power after the 1998 election in Sweden, the Social Democrats have been forced into an unholy alliance with the former Communist party.

Local Government

Local governments administer the many shires and boroughs that make up Britain. The function of the local government is to run services, such as health, refuse collection and the maintenance of local streets and community facilities.

Under the Conservatives after 1979, power was stripped from local government and transferred to Westminster. Taxing powers of local government, in particular, have been drastically reduced. In 1975, local government taxes accounted for 11.1% of the total tax collected in the country. By 1996, the proportion had fallen to 3.8%. While local government continued to provide core local services, local government policy was increasingly directed by the national government.

The 1988 Education Act set curriculum standards that had hitherto been the province of local councils. The 1994 Criminal Justice Act transferred control of police to the central government. Responsibility for local housing has been transferred to central government run trusts. The politically powerful Greater London Council and the urban councils of other major cities were abolished by the Conservatives as being too Labour dominated. In its place, at the end of 1996, London was administered by 272 quangos.

The emasculation of the power of local councils has, and still does, offer opportunities for business. Virtually all the operations previously run by councils, from garbage collection to street repairs, are now put out to tender to the private sector.

Devolution

Rivalries preoccupying the countries of the United Kingdom have never really been put to rest. The strength of independence movements, such as the Scottish Nationalist party and the Welsh Plaid Cymru, has increased in recent years. Currently, movements are afoot, through a policy known as "devolvement", to give Scotland, Wales and Northern Ireland more independence as semi-autonomous regions. The proposal is to set up another layer of government by forming Welsh and Scottish Parliaments. Northern Ireland already has its own Parliament at Stormont in northern Belfast. Based on votes at the 1997 election, the Scottish National party was the second biggest party in Scotland after the Labour party. The agenda of the Scottish National party is to establish Scotland as an independent nation.

Under present arrangements, both Scotland and Wales are subsidised by England. The protagonists of devolvement may well be worse off economically if they succeed in attaining their objective of spinning off Scotland and Wales as separate

Devolution—What the Scottish Say They Want

In mid-1998, opinion polls taken in Scotland asked whether people favoured establishing a separate Scottish Parliament and if so, what sort of Parliament it would be. The results are as follows:

- Those in favour of independence for Scotland: 51%
- Those against: 38%

But when asked if they wanted to separate from England, the Scottish hedged their bets:

- Those in favour of a Scottish Parliament with Scotland remaining part of Britain: 58%
- Those who favoured an independent Scotland separate from Britain: 34%

Like most such surveys, the result depends largely on the phrasing to the question rather than some deeply held belief.

Poll Sources: System Three, ICM

administrative entities. However, the prospect of becoming a Scotsman or a Welshman rather than a Briton is an atavistic notion that appeals to the heart rather than the mind. People of Wales and Scotland place great store in their tribal roots. In the long term, the Scottish Nationalists propose that Scotland separate from England completely and become a full member of the EU in its own right.

Companies in Scotland and Wales are less enthusiastic about devolution. Some business people pay lip service to the idea. Others openly oppose it. The main sticking point is that Scotland, Wales and Northern Ireland are all economically dependent on England. The economy of Britain is heavily regionalised. The bulk of the nation's wealth is generated in southern England, particularly in the south-east, centred around the capital, London.

Many businesses in Scotland and Wales obtain direct subsidies and other concessions for locating in depressed decentralised areas. Devolution, if it were to occur, could threaten these arrangements. A 1996 survey found that the London economy subsidises the rest of the country by about £6 billion per year.

Moreover, business people have pointed out that creation of separate governments in Scotland and Wales may do little more than create another level of bureaucracy between themselves and the government in London—as is already the case in Northern Ireland. Despite the reservations, a Scottish Parliament was formed in Edinburgh in May 1999.

The boundaries of modern day Britain were drawn in 1922, following the departure of southern Ireland from the United Kingdom. Some view the loss of Eire as the first step in the gradual disintegration of Britain into its constituent countries. Like Yugoslavia, Britain may well, sometime in the future, revert to its historical boundaries of England, Scotland and Wales—with Northern Ireland returned to the Irish. It is conceivable, therefore, that an investor setting up business in the United Kingdom could one day find his or her business under the administration of the government of one of the constituent countries.

Northern Ireland

Northern Ireland is the most independent of the constituent countries of Britain. Businesses setting up shop in this part of the world should check local legislation. Areas in which Northern Ireland laws differ from those of the rest of Britain include corporate formation, rules on the environment and rules on the employment of labour.

Foreign Investment in Britain

The British have a strong belief in the freedom of trade and ownership. The country actively encourages foreign investment. As a consequence, Britain is one of the easiest countries in which to establish a foreign-owned business. There are no restrictions on capital transfers or repatriation of dividends. There are no exchange controls or restrictions regarding foreign shareholders on the corporate register of any company. Other than a few restrictions in areas like media ownership, foreign individuals and foreign companies are free to participate in the economy and enjoy the same rights as domestic companies.

Foreign investment plays a very large role in the British economy and is actively encouraged by the government. Of the world's economies, the absolute amount of foreign investment into Britain is second only to that into the United States. According to a 1998 Invest in Britain survey, investment in Britain accounts for 40% of total US overseas investment. In addition, 40% of Japanese investment in the EU goes to Britain.

Taxation

Like any country, the British government engages in an ongoing battle to balance its budget. In the 1980s and 1990s, under its privatisation programme, the Conservative government transferred a good deal of economic activity to the private sector. This was balanced by an increase in the cost of government over the same period—in particular, the cost of social welfare to an ageing society.

The net effect of these opposing forces has been that government expenditure as a percentage of GDP has risen slightly over the period. In 1996, taxation in Britain represented 36% of GDP compared to an average of 40.8% for OECD European countries. The comparative figure for the United States was 28.5% and that for Japan was 28.4%.

Financial Year

In Britain, the tax year for individuals begins on 6 April and ends the following 5 April. The tax year for companies is from 1 April to the following 31 March. Companies may operate accounting years that differ from this tax year, with the preponderance of companies using the calendar year—1 January to 31 December. The accounting year selected is the option of the company. Different accounting years suit different industries. For example, few retailers end their year on 31 December because companies are immersed in the Christmas period at this time, which is usually their busiest time. Likewise, few companies will end their year on 31 March because, depending on the lunar calendar, two, one or no Easters may fall inside a particular accounting year, distorting trading comparison between successive years.

Administration of Taxation

Taxation in Britain is administered by the Department of Inland Revenue. From the point of view of a foreign investor, liability to British taxation is greatly influenced by the British residency status, or otherwise, of the individual or the corporation.

Corporations and individuals residents in Britain pay British tax on worldwide earnings. Corporations and individuals not resident in Britain pay British tax only on income earned in Britain.

British Taxation Mix
Based on 1997 figures, the total British tax take is split as follows:

	Percentage of Total
Personal income tax	41
Value added tax	26
Excise duties	17
Corporate income tax	13
Stamp duty	1
Capital gains tax	1
Inheritance tax	1
Total	100

In addition, local authorities, raise taxes through levies, such as council rates and various license fees, which businesses establishing in Britain may be required to pay.

Definition of what constitutes residency in Britain for tax purposes is long and complicated and greatly influenced by case law. Since British citizens working overseas can save on taxes by arranging their affairs to avoid British residency, a great deal of accounting effort has gone into devising non-residency schemes for British citizens. For this purpose, a thriving financial industry offering offshore accounts has been established in the tax havens of the Isle of Man and the Channel Islands.

Britain is party to international tax treaties with at least 80 countries. Existence of a double tax treaty with the investor's domestic country generally acts to protect the overseas investor from inequities, such as double taxation. Investors from tax treaty countries will also obtain relief from withholding tax. Provisions of double taxation treaties are complex and specific to each country. The particular tax treaty with the investor's country of origin will determine the investor's liability for British tax

Personal Income Tax

Britain operates a PAYE ("pay as you earn") tax collection system for wage and salary earners. Tax is levied on a sliding scale where the percentage of tax payable increases with income. The top personal income tax rate is 40%. Tax deductions are allowed for a small range of expenses, such as interest on home mortgages.

Taxpayers whose sole income is from wages and salaries are not obliged to file a tax return. Taxpayers earning income other than from wages and salaries or earning income in addition to wages and salaries can opt either to file an annual tax return or have the Department of Inland Revenue compute their tax. Personal tax returns for the year ending 5 April must be filed before 31 January the following year.

Companies hiring more than a nominal number of employees are obliged to collect tax from the pay packets of their employees. Each month, companies must remit to the Inland Revenue the total of PAYE tax collected. Very small companies can remit their tax payments less frequently. Inland Revenue provides a code number against each employee to enable the employer to collect the correct amount of tax. Most proprietary off-the-shelf accounting software available for sale in Britain comes pre-programmed with income tax calculation formulas. All the employer has to do is make a once only entry of the employees' tax codes.

Value Added Tax

Value added tax in Britain is widely known by the acronym, VAT. The British system for assessing VAT is the same, in principle, as that applied throughout the rest of the European Union, with each EU country adding its own peculiarities to the fundamental idea.

The detail of VAT may be a little more complicated, particularly where imports and exports are involved. For example, VAT treatment varies depending whether or not the source of imports and the destination of the exports is an EU country. Some goods and services are exempt from VAT, such as food, insurance,

VAT—A Summary
The essence of VAT is as follows:

- When a company buys its raw materials from a supplier, the price paid to the supplier includes a VAT charge raised by the supplier. This, in relation to the purchaser, is called "input tax".
- When the company sells its product to its customer, the price charged includes a VAT charge raised by the business and paid by the customer within the price of the goods. This is called "output tax".
- Since the business is adding value to the goods, the selling price will be greater than the price paid for raw materials. Therefore, the output tax will be greater than the input tax
- The difference between output tax and input tax is remitted as VAT to the Customs and Excise Department.

banking services and education. In addition, some input taxes are not deductible against corporate income tax, such as VAT on business entertaining expenses and VAT on motor cars purchased for the corporation.

VAT in Britain is administered by the Department of Customs and Excise. Businesses making goods in Britain that are subject to VAT need to register themselves with the Department of Customs and Excise as VAT-paying entities (unless the value of the goods made is less than the registration limit of £45,000). VAT is paid quarterly. There are a few situations where a company is entitled to rebates of VAT (where products are zero rated but VAT is paid on inputs). In this case, the company is entitled to receive monthly rebates of VAT from the Department of Customs and Excise.

Full details of the rules and regulations relating to VAT can be found in explanatory handbooks provided by the Department of Customs and Excise.

Excise Duties
Excise duty is charged on items such as fuel, alcoholic drinks and tobacco products.

The manufacturer collects excise duty within the price paid for the product and remits it to the Department of Customs and Excise. The rate of excise varies from product to product and from time to time.

Corporate Income Tax
Prior to distribution, tax is charged on corporate profits as dividends. In 1997, the main rate of corporate tax was lowered from 33% to 31%—one of the lowest rates in the EU. To further encourage venture capitalists, smaller companies are offered additional concessions. Companies making less than £300,000 profit are taxed at 21%. Companies making profits of between £300,000 to £1.5 million is taxed on a sliding scale between the concessional rate of 21% and the full rate of 31%.

Further reduction of corporate tax is on the cards. The Labour's 1997 election manifesto promising a starting rate of 10% tax for high-tech start-up ventures had not been fulfilled by the end of 1998 but is still a possibility for the future.

Britain operates an imputation system on share dividends. Inland Revenue recognises that corporate income tax has already been levied on profits distributed to shareholders. Tax paying individuals receiving shareholder income will therefore receive a tax credit for the amount of corporate tax already paid prior to distribution of dividends.

Companies are required to file tax returns at the end of the tax year showing an income statement to an approved UK standard. Accepted accounting standards are those set out in Statements of Standard Accounting Practice (SSAPs) issued by professional accounting bodies. Internal Revenue operates a voluntary assessment policy whereby companies are responsible for lodging their own tax returns. Most companies employ the services of a taxation agent. Fees charged by taxation agents depend on the complexity of the return but are generally not excessive. Returns must be filed within 12 months before the end of the accounting year to avoid a late return penalty. Based on the tax return submitted by the company, Inland Revenue will make its own assessment of tax to be paid. Tax is payable within 30 days of the date of this assessment.

If a company considers tax to be over-assessed, the matter may be resolved with the local Inspector of Taxes. Failing a successful resolution, a corporation has the option of having its case heard through the court system. This requires the services of barristers and professional accountants and is likely to be expensive.

Though the tax system operates through self-assessment, Inland Revenue has the right to demand an audit. In the event an audit is conducted, Inland Revenue may require supporting documentation to substantiate tax returns up to six years back. Companies must therefore keep all their accounting records for at least this period.

Stamp Duty

Stamp duty is payable on sale and lease of land and buildings. The rate of stamp duty is in the range of 0.5% to 1.5% of the value of the transaction and can be assumed to average 1% for most transactions.

Capital Gains Tax

Capital gains tax for companies is levied at the rate of corporate income tax. For individual capital, gains taken within the tax period are added to income and taxed at the marginal tax rate.

Inheritance Tax

The basic inheritance tax rate is 40% and applies, with some exceptions, to inheritances over £150,000. The steep rate of tax has motivated some people to divest themselves of assets before reaching the age where they consider they are likely to die. The authorities recognise this practice of divestment and will levy inheritance tax (at a reduced rate) on assets divested up to seven years prior to the death of the testator.

Windfall Tax

Under the programme to privatise government utilities, a tax was introduced to recover any excess profits that might be made on the appreciation of the shares of the companies being privatised.

Local Government Taxes

One of the major objectives of the Conservative government of the 1980s was to make local authorities self-funding. Before the Conservatives came to power, local government revenues were insufficient to meet the costs of local government services, such as education, health, garbage collection and street repair. Substantial supplementary central government funding was needed to make ends meet.

Poll Tax

Pursuing its election mandate to balance the budgets of local government, the Conservatives levied the community charge, which became more commonly known as *poll tax*. This was possibly the most radical social programme of the modern Conservative era. The objective of poll tax was to recover the cost of running the municipality from all its citizens—not merely property owners. Users of local government services had to pay for them.

This concept was the ultimate expression of the "user pays" principle. Despite years of Thatcherism, the notion of a cradle-to-grave welfare system has been deeply rooted in the community and poll tax provoked outrage amongst disadvantaged groups—the unemployed, the sick and various others conditioned over the years to anticipate a lifetime living off the state. There were riots in the streets and burning of political effigies.

Thatcher stuck to her guns for a while but ultimately, poll tax failed because it proved impossible to collect. Property rates were reinstated as the primary source of local government revenue and the services of local government were cut to achieve the desired balance between revenue and cost.

Transfer Pricing Agreements and Anti-tax Minimisation Provisions

Britain is party to international transfer pricing treaties designed to prevent tax avoidance through artificial transfer pricing schemes between affiliated companies. In the case of trade within the EU, if artificial transfer pricing schemes are suspected between branches of international companies, Inland Revenue *may* disclose information included on a corporation's tax return to tax authorities of other countries in the EU. In this context, prospective investors are alerted to a ruling by the House of Lords in relation to tax minimisation through artificial pricing agreements of subsidiaries of international companies.

> **Tax Minimisation—A Step Too Far**
> "Where steps which have no commercial purpose apart from the avoidance of tax are inserted in a preordained series of transactions, they are to be disregarded for tax purposes"
>
> — House of Lords ruling, 1984

Summary

As a politically stable country, Britain is a safe destination for overseas investor. Eight centuries after it all started, the British political system is still developing. The move to a single Europe will transfer to the continent some political power previously exercised by Westminster. Hereditary peers are likely to lose their right to sit in the House of Lords, which perhaps will gain more powers as a house of review. The first steps towards a mild form of proportional representation will be taken in 1999. This may slightly weaken the centralised power of the ruling party. Devolution is also on the political agenda. There is a faint chance that the countries comprising Britain will revert to historical boundaries. If that ever happens, in all likelihood, business prospects will probably be unaffected. If it secedes, Scotland has declared that it intends to continue as a member of the EU in its own right. Britain has reciprocal tax agreements with about half the countries of the world, including all the major powers. Tax rates are not excessive by OECD standards. Capital and dividends can be repatriated without restraint.

CHAPTER 4

The British Economy

Overview

With the election in 1997 and 1998 of socialist governments in three of Europe's largest economies, Britain, France and Germany, EU economic direction shifted by the end of 1998. Under previous conservative regimes, all three countries had been pursuing policies of supply side reform and market economics. But in a world where economic fashions wax and wane like the hemline, at the end of the millennium, supply side economics was out and demand management was back in. The coterie of new EU leaders seem likely to pursue neo-Keynesian measures that place greater emphasis on reducing unemployment than reducing public expenditure. What this will do to the zero inflation objective that prevailed in the 1980s and whether Britain, for one, will resume its acquaintanceship with the unhappy days of the 1970s economy has yet to be determined.

As measured by GDP, Germany, France, Britain and Italy are the most populous countries of western Europe and have the largest economies. This is not to say, however, that the larger economies are the wealthiest on a per capita basis. The fact is that the smaller countries of Europe report higher per capita incomes, with the list headed by Luxembourg and Switzerland. On this basis, Britain ranks 18th of the OECD countries, with GDP per capita in 1996 at US$19,241 based on the prevailing exchange rate at the time and US$18,363 based on purchasing power calculations. These figures placed Britain's per capita GDP at about 10% below the OECD average.

Wealth in Britain is unevenly spread across both the country and the community.

Data from the Office of National Statistics showed that for 1996, per capita incomes in the south-east of the country—the "home counties" centred on London—were 36% higher than the national average. Against this, prices, particularly of accommodation, are higher in the south-east, where the cost of living is about 20% higher than the north.

The gap between the rich and the poor of British society is widening. During its socialist heyday, income distribution in Britain was spread more evenly than most countries. This is no longer the case. Income of the bottom sixth of the population declined in real terms between 1979 and 1991, whereas income of the top 10% of the population rose by about 50%. Many other statistical measures of widening economic inequality come broadly to the same conclusion.

In terms of the impact on the prospective investor, within the overall economy, markets for "upper end" products are increasing much faster than the market for staples.

The British Economy

Britain was the world's first modern industrial economy. It belongs to about 80 political and economic organisations. It was also a founder member of the United Nations and one of the five permanent members of the Security Council. Among other economic affiliations, Britain is also a founder member of the G7 group of developed nations, a member of the International Monetary Fund (IMF) and a member of OECD.

With a long history as a trading nation, Britain has long been a champion of free trade. Britain was a founder member of GATT (General Agreement on Tariffs and Trade), the predecessor to the WTO whose *raison d'être* is to promote free trade between nations.

Real GDP in Britain has increased at about 2% per annum over the last 20 years—about the average for countries in the OECD. Year to year variations in the rate of growth during that period ranged from a high of 5% real growth in 1988 to a low of

Gross Domestic Product of Britain by Sector
(1996 figures)

Sector	1986 Percentage of GDP	1997 Percentage of GDP
Agriculture, forestry and fishing	2.0	1.8
Mining, quarrying, oil and gas	4.1	2.7
Manufacturing	24.8	21.1
Electricity, gas and water supply	2.9	2.1
Construction	6.1	5.2
Wholesale, retail, hotels and restaurants	13.9	14.5
Transport, storage and communications	8.3	8.4
Financial industry (including real estate)	10.1	11.8
Rent	7.3	9.9
Public administration, defence and social security	6.9	5.9
Education, health and social work	9.6	12.8
Other services	4.1	3.8
Total	100.0	100.0

Source: Office of National Statistics

-2% in the recession year of 1991. Projections for the next few years are a continuation of 2% growth rates.

The British economy is diversified over a wide range of economic activities, with a shift—shared by many countries—away from manufacturing, the country's traditional industry, and towards the tertiary sector.

World Trade Statistics

The conclusion drawn from the 19th century theory of the Competitive Advantage of Nations advanced by English economist David Riccardo is that tariffs do not pay. Most countries have adopted this view in setting their trading policies. In today's global village, specialisation of economic activity for nations is in vogue and tariff protection is out. Most nations have joined trading alliances, such as the EU.

As trade barriers tumble under pressure of organisations such as the WTO (World Trade Organisation), global trade is expanding at a rate never seen before. The value of goods and services traded between nations is increasing about twice as fast as the rate of growth in aggregate global economic output.

The largest single factor expanding world trade at present is the rapid development of global corporations. Large multinational companies produce different components or brands in different countries. An estimated one-third of all international trade is the trade of products and components between the international branches of the same company. Given the present unremitting pace of globalization, rapid expansion of this sector of international trade is projected to continue. The importance of the external trade sector in the national accounts increases each year for most countries—Britain is no exception. Opportunities to trade with the country increase year after year.

British Trade Statistics

Britain is presently the world's fifth largest trading nation, accounting for about 5% of total global trade. The proportion of British trade to domestic production is about the average for OECD nations. The ratio of exports to GDP is about 25% and increasing. However, on balance, imports have risen faster. The last year in which Britain had a visible trade surplus (excess of exports over imports) was 1983. This was compensated until 1986 by a surplus on the invisible account (excess of export over imports of non-goods services, such as insurance and banking), so that, until this time, the country had an overall current account surplus. For most years since 1987, Britain has been running a current account deficit of about 1% of GDP.

Trade by Sector
Though production of manufactured goods in Britain has declined as a percentage of GDP, the manufacturing sector has retained its importance in the trade account. The majority of British imports and exports are manufactured goods.

Trading Partners
The majority of British trade is now with other European countries. Though the British public has yet to endorse the loss of national sovereignty that full European membership entails, European economic integration is happening anyway. The predictions of Lord Jenkins and other Europhiles of the early 1970s that Britain should turn its back on the Empire and cast its lot with Europe,

British Trade by Sector (1997)

Sector	Exports (Percentage of Total)	Imports (Percentage of Total)
Food and live animals	3.3	7.9
Beverages and tobacco	2.6	1.6
Crude materials (wood pulp, etc.)	1.5	3.8
Fuels	7.3	3.8
Chemicals	13.4	10.1
Manufactures and machinery	70.7	72.2
Others	1.2	0.6
Total	100.0	100.0

have proven correct. British industry has found a niche in Europe that would probably never have developed under previous trade allegiances with Commonwealth countries. Nonetheless, the rest of the world is still important in the external trading account. In fact, Britain runs a deficit on trade within the EU and a slight surplus with non-EU countries.

British Trade with the Rest of the World (1997)

Region	Exports (Percentage of Total)	Imports (Percentage of Total)
European Union	57.4	55.7
Other European countries	4.4	5.5
North America	13.4	13.7
Other OECD countries	6.5	7.2
OPEC	4.8	3.4
Rest of the world	13.5	14.5
Total	100.0	100.0

Sterling and the Exchange Rate

The currency of Britain is the pound sterling. During the 20th century, the sterling has suffered periodic bouts of weakness interspersed with less frequent periods of strength. Since 1980, the sterling has had a roller-coaster ride against the major currencies. It weakened in 1984 during the height of the miners' strike, strengthened dramatically the moment the strike was settled in favour of the government, drifted down again in 1993 on balance of payment pressure, then rose in 1998 under the influence of high interest rates. By 1996, the US dollar/sterling exchange rate was about £1.00 to US$1.66, approximately the same level as a decade earlier.

Any change in the currency, whether a weakening or a strengthening, is customarily termed a "crisis" in the British press by some sectors of the economy. Importers like to see the currency strong, while exporters and industries competing with imports like it weak. The general public is mostly on the side of the importers. A strong pound means cheaper prices at home and cheaper holidays abroad.

The Old Lady of Threadneedle Street

The central bank of Britain is the Bank of England, nicknamed The Old Lady of Threadneedle Street, in reference to its street address. The bank was established in 1694 by a group of businessmen, headed by a Scotsman William Paterson.

The square mile or so around Threadneedle Street, an area referred to by the British business press simply as "The City",

The Bank of England, the Stock Exchange and other major banks and financial institutions are located on Threadneedle Street, the financial hub of London.

contains the offices of almost all the major finance bodies and companies in Britain. Next door to the Bank of England is the Stock Exchange. Down the street and round the corner in places such as Lombard Street are the headquarters of most major British banks—plus a generous sprinkling of foreign banks.

During the last years of the Conservative government, the Bank of England was criticised for lacking independence from government policy. In 1997, the new Labour government addressed this problem by authorising the Bank of England to set interest rates—hitherto a task that had been performed by the treasury.

The principal responsibilities of the Bank are issuing bank notes, regulating interest rates, regulating the money supply, policing the banking system and, in extreme cases, acting as the lender of last resort to commercial banks. The Bank also markets government securities, and pays interest on the national debt on behalf of the government. Another somewhat curious function in an allegedly free currency market is endeavouring to stabilise the exchange rate. In pursuit of this policy, the Bank has attracted its fair share of critics, in particular on the occasions that the Bank entered the currency markets with massive defences of sterling—usually with disastrous results

The Bank of England has attracted criticism for its monetary policy as well. Successful predictions of the interaction between interest rates, money supply, exchange rates, economic activity, investment, unemployment and the other paraphernalia of economics have remained elusive. Over the years, various monetary theories have held sway for a while—and have then been discredited for failing to predict some crises or other. Even in these days of economic modelling with Cray supercomputers, the laws of cause-and-effect remain hard to pin down. There are just as many economic theories out there as there ever were. And an endless supply of economists is on hand to promote their favoured theories and denigrate others.

A Map to the Mysteries of the Money Supply

Economic commentators write about various forms of money, from M0, which is the value of the notes and coins in circulation; M2 which is notes and coins and bank deposits; and M4, which is M2 plus building society deposits. The strange behaviour of the various forms of money is a mystery to most lay-people and perhaps to economists as well.

"The age of Sado-Monetarism has begun. In the corridors of power, they are naming the money supply after motorways—M1 and M2 and M3—the better to map out its mysteries."

— Malcolm Bradbury, *Rates of Exchange*

Inflation

The primary measure of inflation in Britain is the retail price index (RPI). This is the equivalent of the consumer price index of most other countries and is the weighted average price of household expenditure categorised as travel, food, housing, personal expenses and alcohol and cigarettes. Like most OECD countries, inflation in Britain in the late 1980s was almost 20% per annum. This dropped into single digits for most of the 1980s. For the period 1994 to 1997, the average annual rise in the RPI was under 3%.

Even at this level, at the end of the 1990s, inflation in Britain was well ahead of its major trading partners—Germany and France, where inflation was barely 1%. In 1997, the Labour government introduced some mildly expansionary policies in an effort to tackle unemployment. However, most economists, at the end of 1998, were anticipating the onset of a deflationary period, with possibility that the RPI would enter negative territory in the first years of the new millennium.

Unemployment

Unemployment in Britain is not as high as continental countries,

Buskers are common in London, Many are unemployed and entertain passers-by for money along sidewalks and in shopping malls and Underground stations.

A Summary of British Employment Statistics

Unemployment in 1998	5.7%
Average unemployment (EU)	10.6%
Peak unemployment (1990s)	11% (1993)
Average annual growth in employment	0.4% (highest in EU) (1980 to 1998)
Percentage of women in the workforce	46%
Average hours worked per week (1996)	44.5 (down from 47 in 1966)

such as Germany and France. Excess labour, however, exists in most areas and in most occupations. Investors establishing operations in Britain should find little difficulty obtaining a skilled labour force.

Unemployment is spread unevenly throughout the country. Projects locating to depressed areas, such as the Midlands and the north, will most likely find themselves in areas of high regional unemployment, where competition for new jobs is keen. Unemployment is much lower in the southern part of the country.

Official statistics on British unemployment should be interpreted cautiously. Since 1977, the Department of Employment has redefined the term *unemployment* more than 30 times. The stated objective of each redefinition was to increase the accuracy of the definition of the unemployment figure. However, critics of the process point out that all the changes have had the effect of reporting a lower and more politically acceptable unemployment number from a given pool of those out of work. If unemployment statistics were calculated on the same basis as 20 years before, they would be about 25% higher than reported figures. The general view is that, however it is officially counted, real unemployment has decreased in the 1990s.

The nature of the labour force has changed over the years and jobs have been lost in manufacture and agriculture, both of

Percentage of Workforce Employed in Each Sector

Sector	1980	1990	1995
Service	27.8	35.6	36.6
Manufacturing	32.2	23.9	21.8
Construction	5.7	5.1	4.2
Government services	22.4	25.5	27.8
Utilities	8.6	7.9	7.8
Agriculture	1.7	1.3	1.2
Mining and oil	1.7	0.8	0.5

Note: Distribution of statistics between these categories is somewhat arbitrary. For example, services such as healthcare that may be provided by the private sector are included in the "government services" sector.

which have become more automated. Employment in the service sector has grown to compensate the loss of manufacturing jobs. Whether the service sector will continue to take up the slack in the employment market is a moot point. The service sector is itself suffering the threat of job losses through technological developments, such as Internet shopping and automatic teller machines.

Two of the most prominent trends in the employment market have been the growing proportion of women in the workforce and the move from full-time to part-time employment.

Productivity

Labour productivity, expressed as output per hours worked, is notoriously hard to measure. In addition, it can vary widely from one part of the country to the next or from one factory to the next. For example, in the car industry, the labour productivity of Rover's Longbridge assembly plant near Birmingham has long been the bane of its series of owners, whereas Nissan's Sunderland plant in north-east England clocks up the best labour productivity figures

Fleet Street and the Print Unions

International media mogul Rupert Murdoch acquired a broad spectrum of London-based British newspapers in the 1970s and 1980s. His acquisitions ranged from *The Times*—possibly the country's most prestigious paper—to *The Sun* and *The News of the World*, commonly referred to in Britain as the "gutter press".

At that time, print unions had successfully blocked the introduction of new production technology into Fleet Street where virtually all London papers were produced. To preserve jobs that the march of technology had rendered obsolete, print unions were strong enough to thwart attempts by newspaper proprietors to introduce computerised publishing. In the second last decade of the 20th century, Fleet Street papers were still being produced using manual compositing technology from the previous century.

Enter Rupert Murdoch, known by the print unions as "the dirty digger", in reference to his then Australian nationality (he later became a US citizen). Murdoch took time off from his international duties to take personal charge of the campaign to upgrade the production technology of his British papers. The period was 1984 and the success of Margaret Thatcher in vanquishing the miner's union was enough to convince Murdoch that he could successfully take on the print unions. Murdoch built a state-of-the-art newspaper plant away from Fleet Street, at a place called Wapping, on a plot of wasteland that had once been part of the London docks.

When the plant was completed, Murdoch merely moved his operation into a union free "fortress Wapping" (the place had to be heavily guarded for a while) and proceeded to print his papers using computer driven equipment instead of people. The unions tried to boycott distribution of the papers, but without success. The 20th century had arrived in the newspaper industry. Along with the miner's union, the power of the print unions on Fleet Street was broken. Other newspaper proprietors soon followed suit in introducing the new technology.

of any auto assembly plant in Europe.

Productivity is influenced by many factors. Not the least of them is the degree automation of the factory in which it is being measured. Since 1980, manufacturing productivity in Britain has increased at an average annual rate of 1.2%—about the same rate of increase as recorded by Japan, France and Italy and double that of Germany and the United States. However, British labour productivity was coming off a low base. Average productivity in 1996 was thought to be about 30% below the equivalent figures of the United States and Germany.

Reduction of industrial disputation as a result of the Conservative's tough industrial reform programme produced a large part of the productivity increase. Not only have the number of man hours lost to industrial disputes fallen dramatically, but the workforce no longer resists adopting modern productive methods, such as computer technology.

Privatisation

Hand in hand with the new labour laws that the Conservative government introduced during the 1980s—and equally controversial—was the new government's privatisation programme. A major plank in the government's economic policy was to sell off publicly-owned commercial activities. Once elected, the new government proceeded to implement this policy with a vengeance.

During the years that the Conservatives were in government, all public utilities—gas, water supply, the rail system, electricity and telecommunications—were privatised. Also privatised were government-owned commercial operations that were in direct competition with the private sector, such as British Airways. Small sections of the road system have also been privatised and the extent of road privatisation is likely to increase in the future.

The privatisation programme has attracted both critics and supporters. Studies into the economic consequences of privatisation have proved inconclusive.

Critics claim that utilities that have been privatised are natural monopolies and that, since privatisation, prices have risen while services to consumers have been reduced. Critics of privatisation

cite scandalous share and salary packages that executives of newly
privatised utilities have awarded themselves, pointing out that
these private rewards must have been recovered from charges levied
on consumers.

Privatisation supporters disagree, believing that competition
among private operators supplying the same service must produce
more efficient work practices from which cheaper prices naturally
follow in the competitive marketplace. In any case, the prices that
privatised utilities can charge are restricted by legislation. For
example, British Telecom is allowed to raise its prices by no more
than the rate of inflation less 3%.

The success of privatisation has depended on the industry
being privatised and the degree to which the previously
nationalised industries were fragmented after being taken out of
public hands.

For years, British Steel—a remnant from the basic industry of
the Industrial Revolution—required taxpayer support to fund its

aged plants and bloated workforce. Having been taken out of public hands and thoroughly modernised, it has become a highly successful business. By 1998, British Steel was the world's most profitable steel company, the fourth largest in terms of sales and had productivity figures 30% higher than German and US steel industries.

It is generally considered that the privatisation of British Telecom has been successful. Service has improved and costs have reduced. The privatisation of British Rail, however, has been something of a public relations disaster. Train services between the 25 train operating companies (Tocs) that once were British Rail have been difficult to co-ordinate. Incidence of train accidents increased after accountants slashed maintenance budgets of cost conscious private operators. Late arrival of poorly maintained trains became the norm rather than the exception.

After the round of privatisation, industries that remain in private hands are the Post Office, London Transport (the Underground and buses) and the Civil Aviation Authority. Of these, the first two are possible candidates for future privatisation.

Whatever the rights or wrongs of the policy, the privatisation programme is unlikely to be reversed. Even with the change to the Labour government in 1997, this policy remained in place and is likely to continue in the future. Today's Britain is pro-business, pro-free enterprise and likely to stay that way.

Infrastructure

The transportation infrastructure of Britain is the product of 2,000 years of history. The road system reflects the various eras in which particular roads were constructed. For example, the straightness of the old Roman roads in Britain is quite striking when one looks at the road maps of today. Roads left by later societies tended to follow the natural contours of the countryside or, perhaps, the meanderings of the cattle tracks of antiquity.

As it had for the broader-based Industrial Revolution, impetus for development of improved transport came from the coal industry. Transporting coal from mine to market was almost as arduous as mining it in the first place. Within the mine, coal was conveyed by pony and human labour from the coal face to the surface of the mine. From there, it was hand loaded onto horse-drawn carts and taken to the nearest port where it was manhandled onto sailing barges then transported to the markets, principally London, where coal was again manhandled from the barges into sacks then delivered to point of use.

Canals

The first major improvements to the coal distribution system were a network of canals that replaced horse and cart. The 20 years from the construction of the Bridgewater Canal in 1761 saw frenzied canal building that served the coal mining industry until the 1830s, when another frenzy of construction activity commenced—this time, the building of railway lines. In 1825, the first coal hauling railway line opened for business and rail soon replaced canal as the most economical means of transporting bulk cargoes around the countryside. Though the water-borne cargo era has now passed, the system of internal waterways is still in use in Britain, mainly for recreational purposes.

The Rail System

Railways of various sorts were already used in coal mines from the middle of the 18th century. Motive power was initially provided by humans or by horses.

In 1829, the steam engine found its way into the *Rocket*, the first successful mechanically powered railway locomotive, built by inventor George Stevenson. The Rocket, capable of an impressive 36 miles per hour (mph), conveyed coal between a mine in Stockton in north-west England to Darlington, a distance of 10 miles. The first steam powered passenger service was opened a year later between Manchester and Liverpool. Soon afterwards, railway lines of various gauges were set up all over Britain.

To create the gentle grades that railways needed, the *navvies*, gangs of itinerant labourers—mostly Irishmen—excavated cuttings, built embankments and drove tunnels. Engineers, such as Brunel and Joseph Stevenson (son of George of Rocket fame), spanned rivers with bridges constructed from iron and steel, the structural materials of the Industrial Revolution.

The Gauge Act

The result of frantic but uncoordinated activity of the 18th century was the construction of various non-connected privately owned railway systems, with gauges ranging from 7 feet to 2 feet 6 inches. In far-sighted legislation, the government decreed in the Gauge Act of 1846 that all rail lines in the country should be standardised. A track width of 4 feet 8½ inches—that of Stevenson's original Rocket—was agreed upon. This became the standard for the world simply because the British were the pre-eminent builders of rolling stock at the time. Countries building railways set their rail gauge to suit the locomotives that England supplied. As a result, the railways of Britain are compatible with those of continental Europe and North America.

At the start of World War I in 1914, the railways fell under government control. At that time, ownership of the system had been consolidated to four companies and the rail network had reached its peak. After the war, railways came under increasing competition from road transport. The entire rail network was nationalised in 1948 by the then Labour Atlee government. The railways persistently lost money, so the government commissioned a study, the Beecham Report, to find ways to make the system more profitable. From 1958 to 1968, the Beecham Plan was implemented. Half of the 5,000 stations of the system were shut down and rail tracks were removed from uneconomic secondary rail routes.

Currently, the consequences of the Beecham Plan are being cautiously re-evaluated. Closing down much of the transportation system may have been counterproductive in the long run, transferring travellers to the least economically and environmentally efficient method of transportation—the motor car. Some railway stations are being reopened on a trial basis to see if they can make money from rail operations. By the end of 1977, a total of 170 stations closed down under the Beecham Plan had been reopened.

The government's 1996 Green Paper, *Transport: The Way Forward*, found that over the period 1985–1995, rail usage has not changed significantly, while road usage increased 35%. Since then, however, rail patronage has started to increase—by about 7% per annum over the period 1996 to 1998.

The high speed intercity routes are the most used and most profitable parts of the rail network, with high speed trains connecting cities at speeds that cannot be matched by road transport. The speed of the express trains has brought population centres, such as Yorkshire, 200 km to the north, and Wales, 150 km to the west, within commuting distance of London. With the advent of fast trains, the average commuting distance has increased an amazing 50% over the past 20 years.

Rail freight for bulk materials is competitive. There are other forces, too, such as environmental concerns, prompting renewed interest in rail as the preferred form of transportation.

With the opening of the Channel Tunnel in 1994 (the Chunnel), the rail system of Britain is now connected to the SNCF railway system of France—and thereby, to the rest of Europe. Opening of the Channel Tunnel has offered a new option for road freighters to transport their goods between Britain and the continent. Freight companies can use a special rail car service, called Le Shuttle, to transport laden truck trailers through the tunnel and connect them to a prime mover at the other side to continue the journey. Other alternatives are to load the entire truck/trailer onto a ferry or to use standard freight wagons. The relative economics of each method varies according to the product carried and the distance travelled on either side of the tunnel. Prices charged on cross channel ferries, the competitive alternative means of travel, rose sharply at the end of 1998, when the abolition of duty free sales, which had generated half of ferry profits, were scrapped under EU trading rules.

Critics of British Rail point out that the speed of Chunnel trains in Britain is less than the French side and that in 1995, per capita investment in railways was about 70% of the European average. However, overall Britain has been well served by its rail system, which has access to most parts of the country. The high-speed connection between the Channel Tunnel and London is due to be completed in 2002. One effect of the rail connection to Europe has been a vast increase of French tourists in Britain. The French comprise the single largest tourist group in Britain.

The Road Network
By the end of the 17th century, a network of narrow, rutted, unsurfaced carriageways had been built, along which people travelled by foot, horseback or horse-drawn carriage—an infrastructure that was inadequate to sustain the Industrial Revolution that was about to emerge.

The Industrial Revolution opened the minds of inventors and entrepreneurs to innovation in all sectors of industry. Just after the turn of the 19th century, road technology took a giant leap forward. Scottish engineer John Macadam developed methods of sealing gently cambered roadways that immortalised his name in the words *Macadamise* and *Tarmac*. Over time, the rutted tracks of yesteryear evolved into the road network of modern Britain. Road design in the rest of the world quickly followed suit.

The backbone of the British road network is a series of linked dual carriage highways with complete grade separation—the motorways—which connect major population centres. The motorway system (M roads) feeds the non-grade separated system of major roadways (*A* roads) and minor roadways (*B* roads). There are about 2,880 km of motorway in Britain and 7,700 km of *A* roads.

After a series of front-to-rear collisions between involving streams of traffic travelling at high speed through mist and fog on icy roads, the authorities imposed a 70 mph speed limit for motorways. The speed limit on the rest of the road system is 60 mph, 40 mph or 30 mph, depending on the category of road. Unlike other EU countries, British drive on the left-hand side of the roadway. At present, there are no proposals to "harmonise" this minor EU aberration by switching Britain to the opposite side of the street (or alternatively, switching the rest of the EU to the left).

Traditionally, British roads have been funded by the state and can be used free of charge. However, the government has recently reassessed its position on the provision of roads and is studying the feasibility of a number of privately funded road links, the costs of which would be recouped by electronic tolls via a transponder fitted to the user's vehicle.

A preoccupation of many governments has been to wean the population away from its love affair with the car. The government's various economic and environmental interests are to promote public transport. The provincial cities of Sheffield and Manchester have even gone so far as to bring back the electric tramcars of a bygone era. Leeds and Liverpool are also considering whether to reintroduce the trams.

However, tempting people out of cars and onto public transport has proven to be a futile task for any government since the motor car first arrived on the scene at the end of the 19th century. Despite steep petrol prices in Europe, each year, people make more car journeys of greater average distance per trip. The number of passenger miles travelled in EU countries rises by about 2% every year. No measures have yet been devised to reverse this trend.

Air Travel

The rate of growth of British air travel, measured as passenger miles, is about the global average of 6% per annum. Heathrow International Airport, situated 30 km west of London, is the country's main airport. As measured by the annual number of passenger transfers, Heathrow is the busiest international airport in the world. Services at Heathrow, including shopping facilities, are excellent. The airport has four air terminals serving Europe, the East and the Americas. London Underground has a station within Heathrow Airport Terminal, offering a direct connection to the centre of London—a trip time of about 40 minutes, with services every three to five minutes. It also has a mainline rail station to Paddington in the west of London, a trip time of about 20 minutes. The M2 motorway leading into London's west end passes just north of the airport. London is readily accessible by bus or taxi.

London is also served by another large airport, Gatwick, situated to the south-east of the city and connected to the city by a direct rail link and main road. Other major airports in Britain are situated in Manchester, Glasgow, Birmingham, Stansted, Edinburgh, Newcastle, Luton, Belfast and Aberdeen.

Europe's largest airline, British Airways, was a marginal financial operation for many years until it was sold to the public. The flotation of British Airways has been one of the success stories of Margaret Thatcher's privatisation programme. The airline made good profits throughout the 1990s, a period of economic recession when the airline industry was intensively competitive. In terms of passenger miles travelled, British Airways is now the biggest international airline in the world. A number of passenger surveys in the 1990s have rated British Airways the world's best international airline. Somewhat immodestly, British Airways adopted the theme in its advertising, dubbing itself "The world's favourite airline".

Other major British airlines are Air UK, Britannia Airways— which is the world's biggest charter airline—British Midland, Monarch Airlines and Virgin Atlantic—the air line belonging to Richard Branson, Britain's best-known entrepreneur.

A limited domestic air travel market exists within Britain, with the major service from London to Glasgow, at opposite ends of the country. Domestic air travel is in competition with the fast and comfortable Intercity rail services, which have the advantage of taking the passenger directly into the centre of the destination city. Various intercity coach services also compete for the same passengers

Ports and Shipping

In the age before man took to the air, travel into the island nation of Britain was entirely by sea. Over some hundreds of years of its history, England was the world's preeminent naval power. Challenged now and again by other European nations, "Britannia ruled the waves" for most of this period.

At its peak in the mid-18th century, British sailing ship design produced the graceful tea clippers, which raced each other around the world, taking manufactured goods to the east and returning to Europe with cargoes of primary produce, such as tea and wool. The *Cutty Sark*, one of the fastest clippers of that era, presently lies in dry dock at Greenwich, outside London, and is open daily for public inspection.

The importance of shipping continued into the 20th century. Although a steady stream of former British colonies obtained political and economic independence, the country remained an industrial economy, exporting manufactured goods and importing raw materials. Shipping goods remained an important industry. Mass transport of people on gigantic ocean liners, such as Cunard's *Queen Mary* and *Queen Elizabeth*, was a new industry of the 20th century. In the same market but somewhat less successful was the legendary White Star liner, *Titanic*. The importance of sea-lanes was demonstrated during wartime. Convoys of merchant ships crossing the Atlantic in World War II kept the British Isles in supplies while hostilities lasted.

After the war, the docks in Britain became a centre of trade union power. The people resisted modern shipping practices, such as containerisation, on the grounds that the manning levels of ports would be reduced through automation. As labour disputes interrupted cargo flows, Britain lost out to European ports—such as Rotterdam—which were completely rebuilt after the war and kept up-to-date with the latest equipment and technology. Therefore, the British jobs were lost anyway—if not to container efficiencies, then to foreign ports.

In recent years, operations in many British ports have been privatised and the amount of cargo handled by British ports has increased—to a record total of 531 million tonnes in 1996. Major ports are located within easier reach of all industrial centres. In order of tonnage of cargo handled, important British ports include London, Grimsby and Immingham, Forth, Tees, Hartlepool, Sullum Voe, Milford Haven, Southampton, Liverpool, Felixstowe and Medway.

Telecommunications

Britain is one of the cheapest places in Europe to make a phone call—at about half the price for an equivalent service in Germany. The national telephone company was privatised in 1990 and became British Telecommunications plc—more commonly referred to as British Telecom, or simply, BT. The privatisation of BT has generally been thought to be successful, with reports of lower costs to consumers and better service. Prices are tightly controlled by the government. Under the terms of its licence, BT cannot raise prices faster than the rate of inflation less 3%.

In Britain, as in most places at the end of the 20th century,

---

Price Control of Utilities

As an example of the government's control over the privatised utility, at the end of 1998, the Mergers and Monopolies Commission ordered BT to lower the charge for mobile phone calls by 40%—from 25p per minute to somewhere between 15p to 20p per minute.

telecommunications and electronic data transfer were the fastest growing sectors of the economy. A number of communications technologies, optical cable, satellite, land-based cable and land-based microwave relay stations are growing simultaneously at a frantic pace. On the global arena, national companies are forming alliances outside their country of origin to take advantage of the fastest growing area of all—international communications. In this spirit, BT has formed a joint venture with one of the biggest telecommunications companies in the United States—AT & T—and in early 1999, the leading British mobile phone company, Vodafone, announced a takeover of US telecommunications company, Air Touch.

With the development of advanced systems, such as e-mail, Internet shopping, audio visual teleconferencing, telephone banking and interactive television (to name a few of many applications), the amount and type of data people wish to exchange with each other is growing exponentially.

Telecommunications in Britain is essentially a "free for all". It represents an opportunity for new entrants to gain a share of a major emerging market. Orange, the third biggest selling British brand name in mobile phones, was established only in 1990 and now operates in 73 countries.

BT's Market

With the expansion of the definition of the word *data* to include product information, supermarket prices—even the 22 hours of taped conversations between Clinton protagonists Linda Tripp and Monica Lewinski—there would seem to be no foreseeable limit to the market for digital data. Taking advantage of ever-improving data transmission technologies, all telecommunications companies are likely to grow rapidly.

Chairman of British Telecom, Sir Iain Vallance stated, when discussing BT's plans to develop its optical fibre system: "We are retailers of anything that can be converted into digital form."

By the end of 1998, the number of mobile phones was about 11 million. At 16.5% of the population, this level of market penetration is around the average for OECD countries. British Telecom estimates that mobile phone ownership in Britain will be 50% by the year 2001.

Britons are also avid users of the Internet, accounting for some five million households. By the year 2000, 20% of the population is expected to be connected to the net. In addition, Internet is getting easier to use in Britain. The new digital superhighway technology enables subscribers to use the telephone and operate the Internet simultaneously over a single phone line.

The Office of Telecommunications (OFTEL) is the government body responsible for supervision of the telecommunications system in Britain. Amongst its responsibilities is issuing licences for firms wishing to participate in telecommunications in the country. The industry in Britain is one of the world's most open telecommunications markets. So far, about 200 such licences have been issued to about 150 participants and the opportunities to participate in this industry are ongoing.

Postal Services

The Post Office, founded in 1635, is one of the few publicly-owned corporations that have survived privatisation. The Post Office was the first postal service in the world to introduce the prepaid adhesive stamp that has since become the standard method for paying for mail delivery. The world's first stamp, the famous "Penny Black", was issued in 1840.

Postal services in Britain are extremely reliable, with special services called Datapost Sameday provided for urgent deliveries. The Post Office has managed to operate profitably while under intense competition for alternative information delivery systems, such as e-mail and Internet. In addition, there are highly competitive private courier services in Britain to take care of door-to-door delivery of urgent items.

The ubiquitous red post box found on many street corners in Britain.

Electricity

In the 19th century, electricity generation, transmission and distribution developed in Britain as a number of privately owned power companies—an ownership pattern to which the industry has now returned after spending most of the 20th century as an integrated nationalised network, the Central Electricity Generating Board.

According to figures prepared by the Office of National Statistics, power costs in Britain are about the fourth lowest in the EU. Since the industry is privatised, large industrial consumers have some ability to shop around amongst the power distribution companies for the cheapest power supplier. Quality of the power is excellent. Power outages are rare.

Standard voltage is 415 volts for three-phase power and 230 volts for single phase. Higher voltage power, either 6,600 volts or 11,000 volts, may be available to larger industrial users by negotiation. The frequency of the power supply is 50 hertz. The standard electrical plug has three square pins plus an internal fuse. Special plugs are sometimes available to run 120-volt equipment, such as electric shavers.

Electricity was first generated in the UK from coal-fired power stations. In the 1950s, Britain built the world's first commercial nuclear powered generator at Windscale in north-west England. The Windscale gas-cooled reactor was opened by the Queen in 1956, with great fanfare heralding a new age of cheap electricity generation. A total of 12 different nuclear reactors of three different designs were built around the country. However, nuclear power failed to live up to its early promise. Nuclear technology was difficult; problems like the disposal of nuclear waste were intractable and costs of nuclear installations have often far exceeded estimates. In addition, the availability and electrical output of nuclear power stations has often proved disappointing. No nuclear power stations are currently under construction in Britain, and three stations of the early Magnox design are currently being decommissioned.

In 1997, nuclear power provided about 20% of the total power produced in the country. Coal continued to be the dominant energy source for power generation. In recent years, oil and gas-fired power stations have also played an increasingly significant role. Renewable sources of power researched are wind, solar, tidal and wave power, which when combined, supply under 2% of Britain's power. The government is sponsoring various projects with the objective of obtaining 10% of the nation's power from renewable sources by the year 2010. The renewable energy industry is sure to attract continued interest and presents opportunities for technology companies in this sector.

In the 1980s, the electricity industry was privatised when the Central Electricity Generating Board (CEGB) was split and sold by the government into a number of privately owned regional generating, power transmission and power distribution companies. There are presently 33 generating companies in England and Wales supplying electricity to the National Grid (NGC), which is a single entity controlled by the government. Twelve regional electricity companies (RECs) distribute power from the NGC to the customer. RECs operate under conditions of the Office of Electricity Regulation (OFFER) under which prices are pegged to rise 3% less than the Retail Price Index (which means that if the RPI is less than 3% per annum, under the statute RECs are obliged to reduce their prices).

The structure of the electricity industry in Scotland is different from the rest of the country, with single power companies being vertically integrated to include generation, transmission and distribution activities. The structure of the electricity in Northern Ireland is similar to that in England and Wales.

Influenced by its greenhouse gas commitments, the government conducts a policy to encourage energy conservation and reduction. On a consumer level, through its Home Energy Efficiency Scheme (HEES), the government offers grants for domestic projects to insulate ceilings, lag hot water pipes and tanks and to undertake draft-proofing projects. These measures represent opportunities for business producing products in these markets. The government is also interested in fostering co-generation projects and may contribute to costs of studies into co-generation. Details of such subsidies can be obtained from DTI.

Despite energy saving and energy efficiency initiatives, consumption electricity has risen at about 2% per annum in recent years. As a result, Britain is expected to fall short of greenhouse gas emission targets committed at the Kyoto Climate Conference of 1997.

Oil and Gas

In the 1960s, large deposits of oil and gas were found in the seas to the north and east of Britain. Since then, many further finds have greatly increased known reserves.

Britain started converting from town gas to natural gas in 1967. In 1986, the industry was privatised and became the privately owned company, British Gas. Early in 1997, the government instructed British Gas to demerge its gas operations into a gas exploration, production and transmission company (called BG plc) and a gas distribution company (called Centrica plc) and trading as British Gas.

The government wanted to increase competition in the gas distribution industry. By the end of 1997, over 70 gas distribution companies were in commercial operation. This industry, too, is open to foreign participation.

The gas industry is regulated by a government appointee—the director general of Gas Supply—who is empowered to control the price of gas and set quality standards for the industry and grants licences to prospective suppliers.

Water Supply

The water boards of Britain were privatised in the 1980s. Some critics of privatisation claim that the privately run water corporations are not investing sufficiently in water storage capacity to prevent the water scarcities of the summer droughts of the future. However, this has proven not to be the case. An OECD Environmental Performance Review found that privatising the water supply in Britain had improved efficiency and provision of water service.

England and Wales obtain 75% of their water supply from rivers and 25% from underground sources, both of which have been fully exploited. There have been some scares in recent times regarding the capacity of the water supply. Some climatologists believe that Britain's climate is becoming more Mediterranean, with long hot summers and reduced annual rainfall. The driest summer on record occurred in 1976, which exhausted many of the reservoirs. Many parts of the country suffered water restrictions as a result. Fortunately, this climatic event was followed by the winter of 1976–77, which was the wettest on record and completely replenished water supplies. However, a dry spell from 1995 to 1997 severely depleted reservoirs once again. To combat a perceived chronic problem, the government has instituted a programme of water conservation. Measures taken include reducing leakage of the reticulation system by replacing metal piping installed in the last century with polyethylene piping and encouraging consumers to adopt water saving practices.

Scotland and Northern Ireland, on the other hand, have abundant rainfall and water supplies, with Scotland exporting water to England to supplement the supply.

Maintaining the quality of the water supply is the responsibility of the Environmental Agency for England and Wales (EA) and equivalent bodies in Scotland and Northern Ireland. EA administers strict regulations to limit the release by industry of liquid borne pollutants. As measured by OECD quality criteria, water quality in most rivers and lakes in the United Kingdom is good. Drinking water generally meets quality standards.

Sewage

Discharge of untreated waste into coastal waters is an environmental problem currently being remedied. At present, 80% of sewage is treated prior to release to the environment and 95% of properties are connected to a sewer. A public works project is underway to reduce coastal discharges of contaminated liquid effluent with the objective of raising water quality to EU bacteria standards. At present, about 10% of coastal waters have a bacterial count outside EU quality limits.

Responsibility for sewage treatment is administered in England and Wales by the EA and in Scotland by three water and sewerage authorities covering different parts of the country. Sewage treatment was privatised in the 1980s. Prices for sewage disposal are around the OECD average.

Providers of Utilities

Current indications are that the demarcation between electricity companies and gas companies is breaking down. Gas distribution companies are bidding for electricity networks, while electricity distributors are bidding for gas companies. Utility companies see themselves as energy providers. The demarcation may break down further in the future, with companies expressing interest in other utilities such as water supply. The companies of the future will provide a wider range of services to consumers and can then be described as providers of utilities to the geographical areas in which they hold an interest.

Summary

The overall economic indicators in Britain are favourable, with unemployment about half the EU average and inflation low. Corporate profitability is good. Trade between Britain and the rest of the EU is unrestricted. Rules governing trade between Britain and the rest of the world are imposed by the EU. The problem on the external account—Britain runs a small but persistent deficit on its current account—has so far been unresolved. Utilities in Britain are of first world standard and are inexpensive by international standards. Most of the physical infrastructure of the country is in good condition, although the reliability of the rail system still leaves something to be desired and road congestion can be a problem—particularly near the centres of some of the older towns. With the privatisation of utilities and leases for operating utilities continually renewed, this sector presents ongoing opportunities for commercial participation.

CHAPTER 5

Establishing a Business in Britain

Business Climate in Britain

Successive British governments since the 1970s have been firmly committed to the private sector. Britain has established a commercial climate within the country that is favourable to business. Various markets and geographical areas receive direct or indirect government support. Assistance is available on an equal footing to domestic and foreign companies. On the other hand, the government also wants to ensure that business is conducted in an ethical manner. Businesses must, therefore, submit themselves to a certain amount of government regulation.

Government Programmes to Assist Business

Roughly speaking, the country is split by economic advantage between the south, which is wealthy, and the north, which is not. The north/south divide is approximately the line between Bristol in the west and Norwich in the east. North of this line, manufacturing industries predominate. The south is the domain of service industries—banking, insurance and the financial sector.

The per capita earnings of people in the south-east is about 30% higher than the north and unemployment in the south-east is about one-third that in the north. Rust-bucket regions around Glasgow in Scotland and parts of central and north-east Britain are seriously depressed. Industries, such as shipbuilding, steel-making, coal mining and textiles, which once supported the economies of these regions, are in decline or are being modernised with labour saving machinery. This has resulted in high unemployment and attendant social problems.

The population of Britain is not particularly mobile, although significant numbers of people have shifted away from dis-

121

advantaged areas to seek better opportunities elsewhere. Over the decades, the centre of gravity of British population has drifted slightly south. The population of the home counties around London, the south-west and East Anglia has increased, whereas Scotland and Northern England are gently depopulating.

The government's industrial assistance policy aims to reverse this trend by encouraging new industry to locate in areas that have fallen on hard times.

Disadvantaged Areas

Disadvantaged areas are variously called Special Development Areas, Development Areas or Intermediate Areas, depending on how depressed they are. To tempt business to establish in disadvantaged areas, the government has established a wide-ranging programme of investment incentives and concessions. To administer its disadvantaged area policy, the government operates the Regional Selective Assistance (RSA) and Regional Development Grant (RDG) schemes, details of which are available from DTI.

In addition to regional aid programmes, the government operates programmes to revitalise derelict inner city areas. Perhaps

Grant Schemes

Primary assistance available is project grants. To qualify for assistance, a project must be seen as viable, but not so viable that it can go ahead without receiving the grant. The applicant must also show that the project will meet certain guidelines, such as:

- Contributing to the regional and national economy
- Adding to overall economic activity rather than merely taking market share from other firms
- Creating new employment in Assisted Areas or, at the very least, safeguarding existing employment in those areas

Grants are available in any amount up to a maximum of £12 million per project.

the most widely reported of these has been the redevelopment of the London Docklands area into prestigious inner city housing.

An overseas investor can take advantage of these investment incentives, which are offered to overseas companies on the same terms as British companies.

Specific Industry Schemes

Inspired by visions of developing the next Microsoft or Apple, both the 1997 Labour government and its Conservative predecessor have tried to encourage leading edge businesses to establish in Britain. DTI runs a programme, called Regional Enterprise Grants, to support such projects. The twin objectives of this programme are to encourage new high-tech business start-ups and to develop disadvantaged areas.

Silicon Glen

Aided by the government, a computer-based industrial area has been developed. The so-called Silicon Glen is a cluster of computer firms along the M4 corridor west of Slough. Arguably, this development has the highest concentration of new technology of any location in Europe. Britain is the largest producer of software products outside the United States.

In addition to the RSA scheme, there is an additional scheme run by DTI, specifically directed to very small firms, or firms with 25 employees or less. Eligibility criteria are similar to the RSA scheme.

Special Grants

Apart from formalised programmes to encourage business, the government may be persuaded to make special exceptions to assist specific industries. Foreign owned enterprises are not excluded. For example, in 1993, BMW took over the ailing British car company Rover, with the objective of upgrading and modernising the rambling Longbridge assembly plant outside Birmingham. This plant directly and indirectly supplies 50,000 jobs to the Birmingham area through the components industry. In 1998, threatening closure of Longbridge on the grounds of low labour productivity, BMW arm-twisted the British government into providing a £200 million grant package to upgrade the plant.

Loan Guarantee Scheme

Small start-up businesses with no track record are unlikely to obtain finance from normal commercial sources, such as banks and the stock exchange. Alternative sources of funding are available for such businesses, provided they have prepared a viable business plan preferably involving an innovative product idea. Under its loan guarantee scheme, DTI may provide start-up capital of up to about £250,000 on reasonable interest terms for small start-up businesses.

Subsidies for Consultancy Services

The government tries to encourage companies to operate more efficiently and thereby enhance the country's competitive position. Specific objectives are to create employment, increase exports, replace imports and improve the physical environment.

Under this scheme, DTI will meet part of the costs of hiring consultants to advise small business on subjects ranging from marketing, exporting, product design, quality control, business plan preparation, financial and information systems and details of government programmes to support business.

The programme is aimed particularly at small- and medium-sized businesses and is administered by DTI through a network of Business Links that operate around the country. Further information on this programme and the address of your local Business Link office can be obtained through DTI

Local Assistance Programmes

In addition to national assistance programmes run by DTI, there are a host of schemes run by regional authorities or special interest groups, with the objective of tempting private investment into particular regions or sections of the economy.

Some Local Programmes to Assist Industry

The following organisations supply loans for small businesses in rural areas:

Rural loans
Rural Development Commission of England
Welsh Development Agency
The Highlands and Islands Development Board
Department of Economic Development (Northern Ireland)

City Grants
These grants are administered by the various municipalities covering designated depressed areas—57 of such areas have been identified. The objective of city grants is to promote industries in urban centres with high unemployment.

British Coal Enterprise (BCE)
Grants are available to special projects. The objective is to reduce unemployment in areas of abandoned coal mines.

Private Seed Capital

While British merchant bankers are leaders at mergers and takeovers, availability of privately subscribed venture capital is less a part of the corporate culture in Britain than, say, the United States. Nonetheless, there are some places an investor seeking venture capital can call upon. In fact, a minor industry of venture capital firms specialises in providing venture capital to start up businesses. More information on the venture capital industry can be obtained through the British Venture Capital Association. A condition of the venture capitalists is that they participate in the management of the ventures they are funding.

Retail Banks

In the 1980s, banks were swept up in entrepreneurship philosophies being espoused at that time by the Conservative government. The banks lent over-enthusiastically to individuals such as retrenched workers, attempting to finance small business opportunities with their redundancy cheques. In 1990–1992, business suffered a downturn. A problem for this nascent tribe of small business people was that about 60% of the capital the banks subscribed to their enterprises was in the form of overdrafts rather than fixed term loans. Overdrafts could be called in at the whim of their local bank manager. In the early 1990s, when the bank managers lost their collective nerve, the overdrafts were called in and a rash of small corporate failures followed. The bankers have yet to overcome this incident. The retail banking sector is still wary about advancing finance to small business. A loan can be negotiated but the interest rates are punitive—5% or 6% above the base line rate extended to blue chip clients.

EU Schemes to Assist Business

Studies have shown that small- and medium-sized enterprises (SMEs) employing no more than 200 people are more likely than large companies to conduct commercially successful projects incorporating innovative technology. The EU recognises the value of SMEs and has established an SME Task Force to develop policies for small- and medium-sized businesses throughout Europe.

The EU operates a programme to encourage collaborative projects between industry and research institutes in member countries. The scheme is directed at fostering innovation in industries that are expected to exhibit strong growth in the 21st century.

Particular industry segments that have been identified under this scheme are energy conservation projects, marine science and technology, information technology, environmental projects, telecommunications, genetic engineering and projects to develop advanced materials.

In addition, the EU may provide loans to help businesses establish projects in Assisted Areas—similar to the DTI programme. The EU programme operates through the European Investment Bank (EIB). Loans of up to half the capital requirements of the project may be obtained, provided acceptable security is offered as collateral for the loan. Most loans are issued through the European Regional Development Fund (ERDF), which has earmarked around £1.9 billion in funding assistance to private developers establishing projects in depressed areas of Britain.

Regulatory Authorities

Laws governing the regulation of business activities have developed over the years in a fairly ad hoc manner. Thus there are now a large number of laws—arguably an unnecessarily large number—to which businesses must comply. Business laws relate to the proper operation of markets, the protection of shareholders and the quality of goods offered for sale. In harmonising British laws with those of the EU, current British legislation is being redrafted and consolidated.

Regulation of commercial activities in Britain is administered by a combination of government departments and voluntary non-government associations, such as the London Stock Exchange. The objective of both government and non-government administrators is to safeguard the commercial climate of Britain by ensuring that commercial dealings are conducted in an ethical manner.

The principal regulatory authority of the British government is DTI, the body in charge of all commercial matters in Britain. The principal legislation that DTI administers is the Companies Act. This act covers rules of incorporation of companies, disclosure of financial affairs and other rules relating to insolvency. Other regulatory authorities cover more specific areas.

The Director General of Fair Trading administers the Competition Act (1980) to ensure that the commercial market place is working for the benefit of the community. The Director General of Fair Trading looks out for illicit activities, such as cartels, price fixing and restrictive trading.

The Monopolies and Mergers Commission is the body that ensures that proposed mergers are not against public interest.

The London Stock Exchange is a self-regulating body that establishes rules for companies raising equity and loan capital on the stock exchange.

Setting Up a Business

Britain offers a full range of well-serviced locations for almost any type of business being established. Existing factory or office developments and greenfield sites are readily available, particularly in disadvantaged areas. As a densely populated nation, virtually the whole country is within easy reach of first class infrastructure services.

Corporate Structure

Factors to Consider
You should decide on the structure of your intended operation in Britain at an early stage of the project. As a foreign company establishing in Britain, your choice of corporate structures is greater than that for domestic companies. You can form a subsidiary company resident in Britain and subject to British tax treatment, trade through a British branch of your overseas operation, establish a British holding company or you can trade through an agency. The optimum arrangement depends on factors such as:

- The investor's country of origin
- Whether a double tax treaty exists with the originating country
- The prevailing tax rate in the country of origin
- Whether the company is making profits in its country of origin
- Whether the proposed activities in Britain are likely to make an initial loss

As each situation is different, an accountant specialising in British tax law should be consulted at an early stage of the intended project—certainly prior to establishing the corporate vehicle through which trading activities will be carried out.

Forms of Corporate Structure
The most common corporate arrangement in Britain is a limited liability company, of which there are two main types—the private company and the public company. The distinction between the two types of companies is that shares in private companies are owned by private individuals, whereas shares in public companies can be bought and sold by members of the public, usually through the stock exchange. Both private and public companies enjoy limited liability. Generally speaking, shareholders in the business

are only liable for the debts of the business to the extent of their share capital.

Other corporate forms are partnerships, joint ventures and sole traders, none of which fully enjoy the principal advantage of limited liability.

Foreign Enterprises

While an overseas company can legally trade in Britain as if it were conducting business in its country of origin, there is a commercial advantage in establishing an incorporated company in Britain. British companies tend to prefer doing business with British incorporated firms. Consequently, the majority of foreign firms operating in Britain operate through subsidiary companies incorporated under British law. The disadvantages of this approach are minimal since there is no requirement to take on British nationals as directors or shareholders.

Regulations for Forming New Companies

The Companies Act (1985) covers the rules for incorporating companies in England, Wales and Scotland. Companies in Northern Ireland must comply with the Companies (Northern Ireland) Order (1986).

Information that must be submitted to the Registrar of Companies when registering a new company includes:

- Proposed name of the company
- Place of business
- Names of directors
- Names of shareholders and details of share holdings

Once the name of the company has been approved, another round of documentation is required, namely the preparation of the memorandum of incorporation and articles of association.

These two documents are fairly standard in format but details, such as the name of the company, the registered address and so forth, are specific to the company. On payment of an extra fee to the Registrar of Companies, company registration formalities can be expedited so they are completed in one day.

There are two alternatives for preparation of company documentation. The documents can either be prepared from scratch or a "shelf company" can be bought that is already fully formed, registered and ready to trade. A minor industry of company formation specialists exist from whom you can buy "ready-made" company "off the shelf". If you buy a shelf company, all that remains after the purchase is to lodge forms with the Registrar of Companies, advising change of names of shareholders and directors to reflect the personnel who will own and operate the new business.

Once registered, a company becomes a legal entity and can enter into contracts with other companies or individuals and can sue or be sued through the courts.

Rules for Limited Liability Companies

Private Companies   There are no minimum or maximum capital requirements for private companies. Private companies can have any number of shareholders but there must be at least one shareholder. The minimum number of directors is also one. In addition to directors, private companies must also have a secretary who cannot be the same individual as a sole director of the company. The principal duty of the secretary is to ensure that the company complies with the provisions of the Companies Act. To verify compliance, private companies must retain their accounting records for three years.

Public Companies   The minimum issued share capital of a public company is £50,000, of which at least 25% must be paid up. No ceiling capitalisation is specified. The minimum number of shareholders of a public company is two. The minimum number of directors is also two. A public company must also appoint a secretary qualified in accordance with the relevant provisions of the Companies Act. Public companies must retain their accounting records for six years.

Common Rules for Private and Public Companies   After registration has been completed, the Registrar of Companies will issue a registration number to the company. This number must be included on all company stationery, such as letterhead paper, invoices and purchase orders.

Companies must hold annual general meetings, at which the directors present the annual accounts to the shareholders. Shareholders can also opt to call extraordinary meetings. All companies must file annual financial accounts with the Registrar of Companies. The accounts and other records that have been lodged can be viewed by the public. Companies must keep a set of books of accounts at the address of incorporation advised in the memorandum of incorporation. The detail required in the accounts of public companies is more comprehensive than for private companies.

Public companies must have their accounts signed by an auditor who is a member of a recognised accounting body. Recently, legislation mandating the appointment of an auditor for private companies was relaxed to relieve the audit costs on small business. Companies with annual sales of less than £350,000 or net assets of £1.4 million are not required to appoint an auditor.

Branches

While there are trading advantages in registering a company in Britain, many foreign companies setting up their British operations opt instead to establish a branch office of their overseas company. If so, the company is obliged to submit to the Registrar of

Companies copies of documents of incorporation of the company in its home country. If these documents are not already in the English language, they must be translated. In addition, the company must lodge details of the personnel operating the business, as well as its latest set of accounts.

This information is lodged on form BR1, which can be obtained from the Registrar of Companies. Once the application is approved, the branch will be issued with an identifying number that must be included on company documents, such as letterhead paper, purchase orders and invoices. At the end of each financial year, the branch must lodge an English language copy of the trading accounts of the overseas company with the Registrar of Companies.

Joint Ventures

It may suit foreign investors entering Britain for the first time to share their enterprise with a British company. In such cases, the foreign and domestic partners may form a joint venture. This arrangement is particularly applicable to projects that have a definite end date after which further involvement between the two parties ceases. For example, construction contracts to build specific structures are often the subject of joint venture agreements. Unlike incorporated companies, joint ventures are not legal entities. The joint venture is merely a contract that binds the two joint venture partners for the duration of the project. Joint venture partners retain separate legal and taxation identities.

Other Business Forms

The other business forms in Britain are sole proprietorships and partnerships. Sole proprietorships are common in small business. They save the time and expense of incorporating a business with the Registrar of Companies, but have the disadvantage that the owner of the business is not protected by limited liability. A tax disadvantage also exists, where the top marginal rate of personal tax exceeds the corporate tax rate. From a taxation and accounting point of view, a sole proprietorship is essentially indistinguishable from its owner. Unlike an incorporated business, a sole proprietorship does not enjoy a separate legal identity from its owner. There is no requirement for an audit. Inland Revenue, however, expects the sole proprietor to keep a full set of accounting records for the purpose of assessing tax.

Partnerships are prevalent in professional associations, such as law and accounting. Unlike sole proprietorships, partnerships are discrete legal entities separate from their owners. A partnership income return must be lodged by the senior partner. For tax purposes, the income of partnerships is distributed to the partners, who lodge separate tax returns.

Traditionally, the concept of limitation of liability did not apply to partnerships. Partners were liable for the debts of the partnership without limitation and this was a severe disadvantage of the arrangement. To overcome this problem, an alternative arrangement, the limited partnership, was introduced, where all partners, except the senior partner, enjoy limited liability.

There is no restriction on the numbers or nationality of partners to a partnership but large partnerships do tend to get unwieldy. Few partnerships will comprise more than 20 partners but there are notable exceptions to this rule, such as large accounting and legal firms.

European Economic Interest Grouping
A special form of corporate structure is the European Economic Interest Grouping (EEIG). This structure contains elements of a partnership, a company and a joint venture. It can only be used by individuals and companies resident in EU countries. EEIG was established to further the objective of harmonising the commercial interests of EU countries. The intention of EEIG is to facilitate

trading between organisations and individuals resident in different EU member states.

Finance Services Industry

Businesses wishing to set up shop in the financial services industry must comply with additional regulations imposed by the Financial Services Act (1986). The principal purpose of this legislation is to protect investors. The financial services industry includes not only include activities such as managing money on behalf of clients, but also the provision of financial advice.

Corporate Tax Planning

The tax objective in establishing the branch or resident office of an overseas company in Britain is to minimise aggregate tax within Britain and overseas. The optimum strategy will be determined not only by the tax regime prevailing in Britain but also in the investor's country of origin. Within the overall decision of incorporating a branch office in Britain or setting up a company, there are an almost infinite number of shareholding arrangements; each of which will incur a different aggregate tax liability. The optimum arrangement can only be decided on a case by case basis. Aspects to be considered are treatment of capital gains tax, share dividends and imputation credits.

The investor is advised to seek the advice of a specialist in British tax at an early stage of the project.

Transfer of legislative powers to the EU offers further scope for minimising taxes. The EU has not yet harmonised itself to a point where tax laws are uniform across member states. Astute companies that trade extensively between EU member states can take advantage of taxation anomalies, incurring particular taxes in different countries.

Trucking Magnates and Flags of Convenience

Eddie Stobart Ltd is one of Britain's leading haulage companies, with a fleet of 800 lorries operating out of Carlisle in Northern England. The Stobard fleet is renowned for its stylish presentation, with sparkling clean trucks operated by drivers wearing business shirts and ties.

To reduce costs, Stobart and others in the Road Haulage Association of Britain have considered moving some of their business headquarters offshore. In this way, they would be adopting age-old practices of the shipping industry, where a high percentage of global shipping fleet registered is under the "flags of convenience" of Panama and Liberia—countries in which registration fees are low and compliance standards are minimal.

For the road freight industry, similar results can be achieved by shifting the company's business address either to France or Spain, where the annual cost of lorry registration is 10%–15% of that in Britain. Under EU rules, this would not restrict commercial operations in any way. Lorries registered in any member state can operate freely in Britain or any other EU country.

In this way, not only can freight companies save on registration costs, but they can also economise by shopping around for diesel fuel. For example, Belgium and Spain tax diesel fuel at 44% and 41% of the British rate. Britain is not the place to arrive with an empty fuel tank.

The Capital Market

Unlike the United States or Germany, British commercial banks are unlikely to invest in business through the ownership of shares or debentures. They can, however, be persuaded to provide funding through overdrafts, often secured against some specific assets of the business. Clearing banks also invest in the share-market indirectly through their role as investors in the Industrial and Commercial Finance Corporation, a government sponsored organisation, with the purpose of providing medium-term assistance to industry.

Britain offers a complete range of merchant banks, which arrange share issues for public or direct investment. In recent years, the proportion of public savings in pension funds and investment trusts and unit trusts has increased and the proportion owned by individual shareholders has decreased. Investment trusts and unit trusts involve both corporate shares and bonds, as well as a broad range of shares. They are thus a potential source of seed capital.

Stock Exchange

In terms of aggregate market capitalisation, the London Stock Exchange is the world's third largest—after New York and Tokyo. In 1998, the total value of all shares quoted was around £800 billion. The London Stock Exchange is located on Threadneedle Street, almost next door to the Bank of England.

The London stock market has an international flavour to it, with, by far, the world's biggest market for foreign shares—a factor that could influence foreign investors to establish in London. London also has the largest number of international bond dealers.

The popular indicator of the state of the market is the Financial Times Stock Exchange Index (FTSEI), more colloquially known as the *Footsie*. In 1998, along with the more general commercial trend to Europeanisation, the stock market entered an alliance with the Frankfurt Stock Market, with the objective of creating a single trading area for about 300 blue chip European shares.

The process of having your company quoted on the stock exchange for the first time is called *listing*. The Stock Exchange has developed a body of rules detailing the conditions under which they will allow companies to *list* on the exchange. In fact, for interested parties, the Stock Exchange produces a publication called *The Listing Rules*—known to stockbrokers as "the yellow book".

The listing rules include the following:

- Minimum initial market capitalisation is £700,000
- Minimum percent of issued equity capital in the hands of the public—25%
- Company must have traded for at least three years prior to listing

Having listed the company, the Stock Exchange imposes obligations on the directors of listed companies to provide regular information to the Exchange. The objective, once again, is to protect investors by ensuring the operation of a proper and fully informed market. Companies are obliged by the Stock Exchange to keep shareholders fully abreast of major changes to operations, such as acquisitions, divestments and capital movements.

If the Stock Exchange panel is not satisfied that a member of the exchange is complying with its rules, it has two options. It can suspend the trading of shares in the company until it is satisfied with the level of disclosure to the exchange or, in extreme cases, it can de-list the shares.

The Stock Exchange is, essentially, a self-regulating institution. However, the government has formalised rules and regulations in the Financial Service Act (1986). This all-embracing act regulates activities of not only the stock exchange but also the entire financial services industry.

Secondary Market

Smaller companies and others trying to mount start-up operations often cannot satisfy the listing requirements of the Stock Exchange. To provide a market where such companies may have access to capital, an adjunct to the stock market was established. This market was called the Unlisted Securities Market (USM), in which companies could raise capital without having to meet the listing requirements of the stock market.

However, the performance of the USM was disappointing. Financial returns to investors was poor. At the end of 1996, after reviewing USM's performance for some time, the Stock Exchange panel decided to close it down. In mid-1995, the Stock Exchange replaced USM with the Alternative Investment Market (AIM), targeted at young developing companies.

Share Trading on the Internet

Like most stock exchanges in the world, the Internet phenomenon may threaten the comfortable life of stockbroking in the 21st century. Currently in the embryonic stage are stock exchange programmes to enable buyers and sellers to list shares and trade between themselves without a broker. Alternatively, specialised brokers offer Internet services at a fraction of the normal brokerage fee. The market leader in this business is Charles Schwass Equity Trading, which, at the end of 1998, was averaging about 500 new accounts per week. The major retail bank Barclays has also commenced an Internet brokerage service.

Responsibilities of Directors

The responsibilities of company directors are frequently reviewed and revised. In recent years, a series of amendments to the Companies Act has attempted to increase the accountability of directors, both to shareholders and the general community. Company directors establishing in Britain are advised to keep abreast of their changing obligations since these are a moving target. Probably the easiest route to this information is the Institute of Directors (IOD), an organisation whose major purpose is to inform directors of changes to their statutory obligations. In addition, IOD also provides insolvency, career counselling and corporate management services.

Consumer Protection Legislation

Public policy protects the consumer by the proper operation of the marketplace. Over the next few years, laws detailing the rights of consumers are likely to be rewritten and consolidated so as to be compatible with the laws of the EU. The objective of this legislation is to ensure that markets operate in a proper competitive manner, offering the widest choice to the consumer of quality products. It has taken a number of Acts of Parliament to accomplish this objective.

Some Acts of Parliament Prescribing the Rules of Commerce

- **The Sale of Goods Act (1979)**
  Amended in 1994, this act entitles the consumer to goods of reasonable quality. The act requires that the goods be fit for the purpose for which they are sold. There is an implied condition of sale, exercisable by the buyer, that if the goods fail to perform the fundamental purpose for which they have been made or if they are not of a reasonable quality, the seller is obliged to repair them, replace them or refund the purchase price
- **The Trade Descriptions Act (1968)**
  This act stipulates that the goods should be as described in the packaging.
- **The Consumer Protection Act (1987)**
  This act prohibits misleading advertising about prices, prohibits the sale of unsafe products and provides general safeguards to the consumer regarding the quality of the product.
- **The Weights and Measures Act (1985)**
  This act defines the accuracy with which the actual quantity of goods provided complies with the description on the packaging.
- **The Food Safety Act (1990)**
  This act sets standards for foodstuffs.
- **The Medicines Act (1968)**
  This act sets standards for medicines.

Consumer Protection Bodies

A number of bodies represent the rights of consumers. The National Consumer Council is a government sponsored organisation that presents the consumer viewpoint to the government. The equivalent EU body representing the European wide consumer viewpoint is the Bureau des Unions de Consummateurs. Specific regulatory watchdogs under the aegis of the Office of Fair Trading handle complaints against privately owned UK utilities.

Acquisitions, Mergers and Anti-monopoly Provisions

Mergers of public companies must obtain government approval. Prospective mergers must first notify the Director of Fair Trading, who then advises the president of the Board of Trade. Approval to most prospective mergers is granted fairly promptly. However, if the Director of Fair Trading considers the merger to be against the public interest, he or she may refer the proposed merger to the Mergers and Monopolies Commission for adjudication.

The philosophy behind anti-monopoly legislation in Britain is similar to the anti-trust legislation in the United States. The government may intervene in the market to restrict the formation of a monopoly if it is against public interest. A monopoly is defined under the Fair Trading Act as a situation where a single firm or group supplies 25% or more of goods to a particular market. Mergers that concentrate supply of goods may be allowed if countervailing factors in the public interest outweigh the disadvantages of concentrating ownership. However, such mergers require approval by the Mergers and Monopolies Commission.

The Times and The Sunday Times

In 1981, the international media company controlled by media tycoon Rupert Murdoch, the News Corporation, was allowed to buy the *The Times* and *The Sunday Time*, even though the takeover increased his media holdings in Britain past 30% of the aggregate circulation of national dailies. Despite this concentration of media ownership into the hands of a single proprietor, the purchase was held to be in the public interest because the two papers were national icons that were losing money and in danger of closing.

Having to appear before the Mergers and Monopolies Commission to argue the case for a merger is time consuming and should be avoided if at all possible. The commission will typically take six months to make a decision on an individual case, by which time, in the fast moving world of business, the merger opportunity may well have passed. Companies may lobby successfully either

The 1986 Guinness Takeover of Distillers Ltd

The 1980s was an era of takeover mania in Britain and much of the rest of the world. At the time, the City was awash with money that merchant bankers were eager to lend to prospective merger clients. Possibly the most controversial takeover of the period was that of Distillers Ltd by Guinness plc, the internationally known brewer of Guinness Stout. Distillers, a much larger company than Guinness, owned the world's largest collection of brand name Scotch Whiskey, including Johnnie Walker, Black and White, Haig, Dewars and 60 other brands. Guinness had already acquired Bells scotch whiskey, the best-selling whiskey in England. The merger would have given them well over 25% of the market. This was in violation of Mergers and Monopolies Commission guidelines. However, the merger was allowed when Guinness agreed to divest themselves of five whiskey brand names within six months of the date of the merger.

On hindsight, the takeover had all the elements of high drama. Respected City players with political connections right up to the prime minister, were found to have taken bribes (termed in the more gentlemanly parlance of the City as "success fees") to boost the Guinness share price during the period of the merger negotiations. Sir Jack Lyons, who obtained permission from the Mergers and Monopolies Commission in a record ten days by using his influence with Prime Minister Margaret Thatcher, was subsequently fined £3 million and stripped of his knighthood for his crimes in manipulating the Guinness share price. Guinness's then managing director Ernest Saunders also served a jail sentence for his part in the affair. Three other executives were found guilty and paid hefty fines.

to avoid appearing before the Commission or to obtain a favourable decision on the proposed merger.

Anti-competitive and Restrictive Trade Practices

The director general is also empowered to investigate any commercial activity that prevents proper operation of the competitive marketplace. The most common investigations are allegations of price fixing, or collusive tendering. Firms with turnovers of less than £10 million are exempt from this form of enquiry whatever the allegations made, as are firms with less than 25% of their particular market.

With a few exceptions, such as the pharmaceutical industry, manufacturers are prohibited from stipulating the prices at which dealers or retailers supply their goods to the public.

Summary

Britain operates a programme of direct and indirect financial assistance schemes to encourage investment in industry. These schemes work to the advantage of investors and should be considered in deciding the geographical location of a new enterprise.

Raising private capital in Britain is probably more difficult that in countries, such as the United States, where community culture is more entrepreneurial. British banks still operate conservative lending policies. The objective of commercial law in Britain is to establish conditions that are fair to all stakeholders in a commercial transaction—the shareholders of the investing company, consumers and taxation authorities. British law represents a reasonable balance between the interests of the various interested commercial parties. A number of anomalies between British and EU laws still exist and will likely iron out over time through the harmonisation process

CHAPTER 6

Running a Business in Britain

Overview

Once a foreign investor has decided to establish a business in Britain, a location must be selected. The government's programme of decentralisation incentives is one factor influencing the choice of location. However, the advantages of locating at the natural focus of your business activities may outweigh the financial incentives to locate somewhere else. It would be unusual, for example, for a merchant bank to set up anywhere but London. Heavy industry, on the other hand, would be expected to locate in the north, taking advantage of the government's decentralisation programme, a ready supply of skilled labour and a network of suppliers of raw materials.

The Sunderland Plant of Nissan Motors
When Nissan Motor Corporation set up a greenfield plant in Britain in 1986, it chose Sunderland in the north eastern industrial area of Britain. As one of the most economically depressed areas of Britain, the project not only qualified for DTI concessions, but received generous concessions from the local government authority as well. For areas where unemployment is high, a significant business can practically write its own ticket with local authorities for infrastructure deals and tax breaks.

Imports

Tariffs

All tariffs between Britain and other EU countries were abolished on 31 December 1977. Goods imported from non-EU countries are subject to the Common Custom's Tariff (CCT). The Department of Customs and Excise publish a schedule of tariffs attracted by such imports. In a few years, the EU will introduce the tariff reduction programme agreed at the WTO's 1993 Uruguay Round of trade talks. Under this schedule, tariffs on goods from outside the EU will be reduced progressively.

The EU has preferential trade agreements with many countries and trading blocs, including Eastern European former satellite countries, such as Poland and Hungary; EFTA countries, such as Norway, Iceland, Liechtenstein and Switzerland; Mediterranean territories, such as Malta, Morocco and Lebanon; former European countries belonging to the African Caribbean and Pacific (ACP) group; and various developing countries worldwide. Imports from these countries will attract a lower tariff than that paid by the rest of the world. This sometimes brings the EU into conflict with WTO free trade policies.

A Split on Bananas

Long running trade disputes between the United States and the EU occasionally erupt into active hostility. Along with most of the rest of the world, the United States is a vigorous opponent of the EU Common Agricultural Policy, which discriminates against US agricultural products. Anomalies in EU tariff policies occasionally have some odd effects. For example, the EU imposes lower tariffs on bananas from ACP countries than it does on bananas from the rest of the world. The United States sees this as discriminatory. In 1998, the United States threatened to impose 100% tariffs on various EU imports in response to the EU policy on bananas. So far, six years of sporadic hearings have failed to resolve this dispute.

Import Quotas, Tariff Quotas and Ceilings

There are no fixed quotas on particular imports. There are no restrictions on the quantity of products that can be exported to the EU from non-EU countries. Some goods, however, may be subjected to a different rate of tariff, depending on the volume of goods that have been imported into the EU in a given period. The terms *tariff quotas* and *tariff ceilings* describe this concept.

Goods subject to a tariff quota will attract no tariff until a certain quantity has been imported into the EU, after which they will attract a duty at the specified rate. The same applies to goods subject to a tariff ceiling, except that exercise of the tariff is at the discretion of EU commissioners.

Grey Imports

Multinational companies sometimes produce goods bearing the same brand name in various different countries. Seemingly identical goods may be produced in countries inside and outside the EU. Goods manufactured outside the EU are often cheaper than those produced inside the EU. Branded goods manufactured in countries outside the EU and imported to compete against identical branded goods produced within the EU are called *grey imports*. The European Commission has banned grey imports into the EU. However, grey imports from member states of the EU are permitted.

Anti-dumping and Countervailing Duties

The EU is a party to WTO anti-dumping conventions. Dumping is defined as selling exported goods at a price below the production cost in the originating country. If an EU company believes it is facing competition from goods dumped on the EU market, it can lodge a complaint to the EU Commission. If investigators find that the complaint is justified, anti-dumping duties will be levied on the importer.

Countervailing duties are levied on goods that have an unfair cost advantage over EU goods through government subsidies in the originating countries. Countervailing duties will be imposed on such goods to force importers to raise their prices.

Taxation Effects

Whether profits from imports will be taxed depends on whether the trading activity is being carried out in Britain or in the importer's country of origin. If the importer is merely supplying goods to orders sent from Britain and the shipments are made up in another country, no tax is payable on the profits made on goods sold. If the importer has established a branch of its company in Britain or holds stocks of goods in Britain, tax will be payable on the profit from the sale of the goods.

Exports

Export of some goods are restricted. Clearance must be obtained from the customs before restricted goods can be shipped. Prohibited exports from Britain include strategic goods and materials, such as military equipment and nuclear isotopes; certain electronic equipment; live animals; and goods considered to be national treasures, such as works of art.

Export of goods to certain countries may also be restricted. Restricted export destinations include China, various countries of the former Soviet Union and Iran. Exports to countries, such as Serbia and Iraq, are currently prohibited under United Nations export embargoes. Approval must be obtained from DTI before goods can be shipped to restricted destinations.

Export Assistance

The British government spends about £200 million per annum promoting British exports. Assistance is provided under the Overseas Trade Services operation (OTS) administered by DTI. The service provides market information and other information about destination countries, rather than direct financial assistance. Details of the service is provided by DTI and Business Links.

Those in the export business may also use the services of the Exports Credit Guarantee Department (ECGD), which can help to arrange finance and payment guarantees for shipments of exported goods.

Legal System

The legal system in Britain developed from the feudal law of medieval times. Legislation is based on a combination of custom, statute and precedent.

In broad terms, legislation can be broken into two categories—public law and private law. Aspects of public law that are of interest to the business sector include taxation, consumer legislation, sale of goods, environmental legislation, employment legislation and

> **The Overarching Effect of EU Law**
> In 1988, British Aerospace (BAe) purchased British Leyland Motor
> Corporation (BLMC) from the British government. To sweeten
> the deal, the British government provided concessions and other
> benefits to BLMC. These were later found to be in violation of
> EU trading regulations regarding unfair government assistance,
> as they gave BLMC an unfair advantage over other European car
> manufacturers. The courts ordered BAe to pay £110 million
> compensation to the British government on the grounds that the
> concession originally granted was an illegal subsidy under EU
> fair trading provisions.

health and safety acts. Private law relates to dealings between
individuals. The principal area of private law of interest to business
is the law relating to contracts.

The hierarchy of the British court system is fairly complicated.
Scotland and Northern Ireland retain separate legislative powers
from England, and Scottish and Northern Ireland laws are
significantly different from English law. The legal systems of
England, Wales, Scotland and Northern Ireland converges at the
top, where the House of Lords acts as the last court of appeal for
all four entities.

Britain's entry into the EU has compounded legal compli-
cations. The European Court of Justice in Luxembourg is now the
ultimate court of appeal for commercial disputes and can overturn
rulings of the House of Lords, subject to EU legislation.

British and EU law is gradually being harmonised, but the
process is far from complete, particularly in the area of criminal
law. Investors should be especially wary of seemingly valid British
law contracts that might violate EU legal provision.

Legal Agreements
Most businesses will be party to various legal agreements, be they
as routine as lease for the business premises or something more
complex. The culture of British business is to reduce agreements

between business entities to written words. Though verbal contracts are enforceable under English law, the British generally do not enter any but the simplest business arrangements as "gentlemen's agreements" without documentation. A written document that ratifies the terms of the agreement is expected for most business transactions. Some business agreements, such as an order for the purchase of supplies, are routine. Other agreements, such as the preparation of contract documents, may require the services of a solicitor.

Once participating parties have agreed to the clauses of a contract, both parties are expected to follow the terms, even if the terms become disadvantageous to one of the parties. Unlike Asia, where contracts may have only the weight of a statement of intent, in Britain, "a deal is a deal". A party not following the terms of the contract can expect to be threatened with court action.

Getting embroiled in the court system in Britain can be fabulously expensive and should be avoided at all cost. Besides, court action between partners indicates a breakdown of the business relationship. One of the major reasons for writing a contract agreement in the first place is to structure the affairs of business participants to minimise the risk of creating the possibility that disputes will end in court. A clearly drafted contract agreement between parties is a prerequisite to minimising future problems.

Hiring Solicitors

Under the British system, legal work is divided into court appearances performed by barristers and advisory work performed by solicitors.

While the legal system is perpetually under review, with the objective of reducing its complexity and cost, there is a vested interest within the profession to keep the law exactly the way it is. The existing legal profession provides a very comfortable living for its retinue of solicitors, barristers and judges. Since a high proportion of politicians come from a legal background, frequent proposals to reform the law are pursued less than fullheartedly. British law is complicated and it is likely to remain so.

To formulate anything but the most mundane agreement between contracting parties, use of a solicitor is pretty much unavoidable. A good solicitor can help you avoid pitfalls and save you money. A bad solicitor, however, may lead you in circles, cost you money and find an array of imaginative reasons why progress on your project is being delayed.

Take the time to select a solicitor you can work with. Ending relations with a solicitor that you no longer get along with is a difficult decision. By the time you get around to

---

Solicitor Selection Checklist

A harmonious relationship with a good solicitor is an asset to your business. Here is a suggested list of points to consider when selecting a solicitor:

- Is your business important to the solicitor? If your work is low on the solicitor's priorities, you may find after the initial contact that your solicitor becomes almost unreachable. Lack of progress on your project is perhaps the most vexing problem of all in dealing with solicitors.
- Is the legal firm experienced in your type of work? Solicitors tend to specialise. You should ensure that your solicitor has prepared commercial contracts before, preferably in your industry.
- Will the person you spoke to be the one acting for you? After they snare a client, solicitors in busy practices are notorious for handing work out to junior associates with little experience—in which case, you may be sponsoring an on-the-job training exercise for a junior.
- Do you really need a City solicitor? A solicitor with an address in the City may cost three times as much as the one around the corner. Is the extra cost justified? Unless yours is a particularly unusual deal, probably not. The solicitor around the corner is usually more convenient and more likely to stay in touch with you as the deal proceeds.

terminating his or her services, you will most likely have expended a lot of time, energy and money with the solicitor for very little outcome.

The size of the bill can sometimes sour the relationship between solicitor and client. When you enter into an agreement with solicitors, be aware that they charge by the hour. Not many solicitors will give you a lump sum quote for the work undertaken. If pressed, a solicitor may give you a forward estimate of his fee, but this can normally be disregarded. When presenting their bills, solicitors think nothing of exceeding their estimates by 400% or 500%.

In 19th century England, solicitors charged by the word for legal documents. Although this practice has been abandoned, the tradition of long legal documents phrased in archaic language lives on. Documents that enshrine the mysteries of the law rather than impart information are inappropriate for business agreements.

The practice of clouding the intent of a contract document with the mysteries of the Latin language does not have to be tolerated by fee-paying clients. Plain English legal documents carry the same weight as their lengthier counterparts produced by solicitors of the traditional school. Solicitors, and indeed clients, tend to forget that the client, not the solicitor, is running the relationship. When instructing a solicitor to prepare a contract, you are advised to request plain English documents and return for redrafting any documents that wander off course into a thicket of Latin-based lawyerisms.

Ensure that your work does not become the subject of a difference of opinion between your solicitor and the solicitor acting for the other contracting party. In this instance, solicitors for the two parties will exchange terse letters between themselves debating points of law without either of the clients being aware that their project is being delayed. You will even end up paying for the exchange of letters. The way to short-circuit this problem is by direct contact with the other party to the agreement—with or without your solicitor's knowledge (you must expect to receive a certain amount of flak from your solicitor if you pursue this course).

Small Claims Tribunal

To reduce costs, small claims tribunals have been established to settle disputes of less than £500, with an increase to £5,000 currently under consideration. Parties to the dispute put their case directly to an arbitrator without any need for legal representation. A single arbitrator or a panel of arbitrators is appointed to hear the case. If the case is heard by more than one arbitrator, the panel generally comprises an odd number of people so that a majority finding can always be reached.

EU Law

As the legal system is harmonised under arrangements to transfer legislative powers to the EU, laws enacted in a member state may

---

Car Dealerships and EU Regulations

An objective of EU regulations is to free up the marketplace and outlaw restrictive trade practices. This can operate to the advantage of a new business setting up.

Traditionally, car dealerships in Europe had exclusive arrangements with particular manufacturers. Dealership arrangements afforded the manufacturers a great deal of power over dealers. For example, BMW and Mercedes issued sales quotas to dealers and could specify the minutiae of their marketing arrangements, such as fine detailing of signage and showroom displays.

Under 1992 EU regulations, the legal enforceability of exclusivity to a particular manufacturer has lapsed. Theoretically at least, dealers are allowed to offer products of any manufacturer and make their own marketing decisions. In reality, as the monopoly supplier of their product, car manufacturing companies still hold dealers in their power, whatever the regulations might state.

---

be in conflict with those of the EU. If so, aspects of a business contract written under the national law of a member state may be invalidated by European courts.

The Court of Justice sitting in Luxembourg is the ultimate authority for the administration of EU. While there is no formal right of appeal against the ultimate authority of the Court of Justice, where rulings of the EU court unfairly disadvantage a British producer, DTI, may lobby the Court of Justice on behalf of the firm involved.

Foreign Lawsuits

Operations outside Britain may be covered by British or EU law. A few cases have been successfully brought against British registered companies by foreigners whose complaints related to an incident that occurred outside Britain.

The Case of Connelly versus Rio Tinto Zinc

Rio Tinto Zinc (RTZ), the biggest mining company in the world, has its registered headquarters in London. Edward Connelly worked as a maintenance mechanic in RTZ's Rossing uranium mine in Namibia, South-west Africa, from 1977 to 1982. In 1986, Connelly was diagnosed with throat cancer. Connelly claimed his ailment had been caused by RTZ's poor safety conditions at the mine. He decided to sue the company but found that the lack of work practice laws in Namibia precluded the action. Connelly sued RTZ in Britain on the grounds that the company's British registration made his employer liable under British law although the problem had occurred in Namibia. At the time, the principle that a company could be sued for an action occurring in another country had yet to be established. Connelly persisted all the way to the House of Lords, which found in his favour, thus enshrining the right of disaffected employees to sue British registered companies for alleged malpractices occurring on foreign soil.

The decision of the House of Lords on the Connelly hearing has presented the government with an ethical dilemma. On one hand, the country is a signatory to the International Labour Office (ILO) bill of rights that seeks to oppose exploitation of labour in third world countries. On the other, the government does not want to discourage international companies from registering in Britain nor does it want to see a minor industry started in Britain with discontented foreigners suing British registered companies through British courts. The signs in 1998 were that the government would most likely legislate to limit the rights of foreign litigants to bring future similar actions.

Rights of Parties to an Employment Contract

Employers are obliged to provide safe working conditions for their employees. These obligations are legislated under the Workplace (Health, Safety and Welfare) Regulations Act (1992).

The statutory rights of employees are covered under the Employment Protection Act (1978) and the Trade Union Reform and Employment Rights Act (1993). These acts cover such employment conditions as handling of grievances, maternity rights and minimum notice periods. Under the legislation, employees

Employment Package

Outlined below are conditions that may be expected in a customary professional employment package:

- Four weeks paid annual leave (under EU directives on working time, employees are entitled to three weeks holiday—rising to four weeks in 1999)
- Statutory public holidays
- Two weeks paid sick pay (no medical certificate is required for sickness of less than three days)
- Company cars (for senior staff)
- Share option packages (an increasingly common component of the reimbursement packages of executives)

are entitled to receive a written statement of their employment conditions including rate of pay, minimum notice period, hours of work and holiday entitlements.

Under EU harmonisation principles, the provisions of EU laws relating to employment are being incorporated into British law. EU provisions are likely to provide employees further rights to those enjoyed under current British legislation.

Legislation also provides rights for employees made redundant if their jobs cease to exist—for example, through a downturn in business or through technology improvements. A retrenched employee is entitled to a lump sum redundancy payment of between half a week's to one and a half week's pay for each year of service depending on the age of the employee. Legislation also provides grounds for an employee to complain against unfair dismissal. The employee's remedies for unfair dismissal are reinstatement or additional compensation.

Other legislation affecting employment is the Equal Pay Act (1970), the Sex Discrimination Act (1975), the Race Relations Act (1976) and the Disability Discrimination Act (1995). These acts prohibit discrimination in employment on the grounds of colour, race, sex and physical handicap. Legislation also provides that no one can be refused employment on the grounds of belonging to a trade union.

Suggested Guidelines for Recruiting

General guidelines for steering clear of employment disputes are to advertise widely, respond to all applications (at the very least invite a resume from anyone expressing an interest in your position) and keep good records. At the end of the day, the employer still has the right to decide on the right candidate for the job. If the employer's stated reasons for disqualifying a particular candidate do not cite gender, race and physical impairment, then an unsuccessful candidate will struggle to make any case for discrimination.

The best legislation in the world cannot ensure that no one in the workforce is discriminated against. From the employer's point of view, the objective is to survive the provisions of the legislation while appointing the person you want for the position you have in mind.

Apart from specific provisions in employment acts, the general principle of employment in Britain is that the employers and employees are free to negotiate their own employment contracts with minimal interference of the state. With the decline of trade union influence, there has been a move away from collective bargaining. In 1996, about 37% of employees worked under collective bargaining arrangements, with the balance under individual contracts. Collective bargaining agreements are most likely found in large establishments and the public sector. Even under collective bargaining arrangements, negotiation is increasingly conducted at the local level.

Women and the Glass Ceiling

Despite anti-discrimination legislation, statistics suggest discrimination is still being practised. For example, the so-called

Women in Power

Britain has produced its share of influential women. Queen Victoria reigned for a record 64 years over the country's most politically successful era. The Elizabethan period of 1558 to 1603 was also a successful historical period in which England asserted itself as a power in European politics, commerce and the arts. Elizabeth II, the current queen, is a well-respected figure who has reigned for nearly half a century. She is the stabilising figure in a series of scandals that might have otherwise led to the downfall of the monarchy.

One of Britain's most influential woman of the 20th century is Margaret Thatcher, the country's first female prime minister. After the 1997 election, a record number of 120 women had been elected to the House of Commons (18% of the members).

glass ceiling that allegedly prevents women from assuming executive positions is still intact—only about 5% of company directors are women, a figure well below the female participation rate of the workforce.

Labour Cost and Availability

The free market principles adopted by the previous Conservative government removed the protection that some employees obtained from their trade unions. Evidence emerged that low paid workers were being exploited, particularly piece-rate workers in the garment industry. The Labour government has re-instituted a national minimum wage—a principle abandoned by the previous Conservative government. In April 1999, the minimum wage was set at £3.60 per hour

Despite recurrent unemployment crises, the average hours worked per week for those who do have jobs has not varied much over 30 years—around 45 hours per week for men working full-time and 38 hours for women.

An investor setting up in Britain will not have a problem recruiting a skilled labour force. Nevertheless, there are always one or two specialist areas in the economy facing labour shortages. For example, the catering industry is perpetually short of chefs and usually has to look to continental Europe to fill its vacancies. Merchant banks, such as Goldman Sachs and J. P. Morgan, also recruit in Europe for merchant banking positions in London. It is difficult to hire British recruits with sufficient language skills to handle European clients.

Social Security

The social security system is designed to generate sufficient funds to finance the welfare state, including retirement pensions, sickness benefits, unemployment benefits and long-term disability benefits. Employers pay a social security levy up to about 10% of the employee's income. In addition, the employee pays a levy deducted by the employer according to a sliding scale. For foreign employees, liability for the social security levy varies with the amount of time the employee works in Britain and the level of pension and medical cover existing in the employee's country of origin. For low paid employees without separate medical cover, the employer may be obliged to pay statutory sick pay from the fourth day of the sickness up to a maximum of 28 weeks. In 1998, the rate of statutory sick pay was £55.70 per week.

Employer's Organisations

Most industries have employers' organisations that can offer help and advice. The traditional role of the employer organisation was to assist employers resolve labour disputes. With the dramatic reduction of labour disputation issues in recent years, however, employer organisations have broadened the services they offer.

Most national employer organisations belong to the Confederation of British Industry (CBI), an umbrella group for employers seeking advice and assistance in a range of industrial and commercial matters. CBI is the biggest employer group in Britain, representing about a quarter of a million companies.

Work Permits

Citizens of EU countries do not need to obtain a work permit to work in Britain. Curiously, despite all the fanfare of removing barriers to job mobility within the EU, only 2% of the total EU workforce elects to work in another EU country.

Citizens of countries outside the EU will need to obtain a work permit from the Department of Employment. The prospective employer must first submit a letter of employment for a specific job to the Department of Employment.

For people wishing to immigrate to Britain who are denied an immigrant visa through normal channels, establishing a business in Britain may offer a way into the country. If you are applying for residence and cannot obtained residency through any other means, you may apply on the premise of setting up a business in Britain. The minimum amount of business capital needed to support such an application is £250,000.

Training

By the end of the 1980s, unemployment had become a dominant political issue. Opportunities for unskilled workers diminish each year. While many people were prepared to re-train, few skills were in short supply anywhere. With the rapid development of new technologies and the even more rapid whole-scale replacement of workers by computers, re-training of the workforce for what jobs remain became a priority for governments around the world. The policy of training people for jobs that did not appear to exist attracted its share of criticism. But at least it kept the unemployed off the official unemployment figures and raised the general level of skill in the workforce.

British policy on training the workforce has varied with the political persuasion of those in power. Under the Conservatives in the mid-1960s, training or re-training the workforce was felt to be the domain of the employer. In the 1970s, the Labour government that came into power became involved, establishing the Manpower Service Commission in 1973. The principal concern at that time was to tackle various skill shortages that the government had identified. When the Conservatives resumed office in 1979, the Manpower Service Commission was disbanded and replaced with Training and Enterprise Councils, a network of local training bodies funded by local industries to serve their needs for labour. When Labour regained government, the policy on training was modified once again. A new network of National Training Organisations (NTOs) were introduced to supplement the Training and Enterprise Councils. Whether public or private, the objectives of these bodies are the same—to ensure that there are no skill shortages and to render unemployed people employable.

Under the Small Firms Training Loans Programme, limited financial assistance is available to assist small firms finance the costs of their training needs. Details can be obtained from the local NTO office.

The Work Culture

British work culture has changed a great deal in the last two decades. In the 1970s, jobs were considered to be fairly permanent arrangements. Most employees were more preoccupied with improving their wages and conditions than they were about remaining on the payroll.

After winning the 1979 election, the Conservative government set out to implement its new industrial policy. A key objective of the incoming government was to reduce the power of trade unions. In achieving this objective, the government succeeded in redefining the existing work culture of an assumed right to "cradle-to-grave" employment.

Other circumstances contributed to this cultural shift. The 1980s was the era of privatisation in Britain, when commercial operations with the most stable workforce—government-owned businesses—were being sold off to the private sector. A typical first action of the new owner was to cut costs by downsizing the labour force. Jobs in the most reliable job providers were no longer safe bets. Contracting out services also became fashionable. In addition, most companies started shedding staff as computers replaced people in all sectors of the economy.

As a result, labour problems that seemed a permanent feature of industrial life in Britain 20 years ago are now a thing of the past. Employees are today more concerned about hanging on to the jobs that they do have than they are about improving their working conditions. Industrial disputation has dropped dramatically. In terms of the rights of the wage earner, OECD rates Britain the second lowest of its members—ahead only of the United States. Less than a third of the British workforce belong to a union. In most areas, labour is in oversupply. Britons in most occupations are ready and willing to go to work—mostly on terms determined by the employer.

By 1990, the full-time job market had shrunk. In 1997, compared to figures in 1977, jobs available decreased by 20%. Less than 40% of the adult population was in permanent employment. Casual work, contract work, part-time work and self-employment had replaced regular jobs.

Normal Terms of Business

Most business in Britain is conducted on credit. Normal terms of business are 30-day payment. This rarely means that money will be seen within 30 days of the date on the invoice. Normal practice is to pay 2 months after the debt was incurred, meaning that money arriving within 60 days will be regarded as payment within the current period.

Collecting money from delinquent payers can be an expensive procedure, due to high costs in the British court system. The government recognises that the payment of commercial debt is a problem in Britain—particularly among small businesses, which are reluctant to chase money for fear of offending important customers. The latest attempt to assist claimants is the Late Payment of Commercial Debts (Interest) Act (1998). Under this act, firms are legally entitled to collect interest on late payments. Firms can opt to enforce this right.

Many businesses use factoring companies specifically to avoid unpleasant confrontations with customers over late payments.

Metric Units

The imperial system of units originated in Britain. It was gradually systematised from haphazard origins that produced units of length, such as inches, feet, yards, rods, perches, chains, furlongs and miles, and units of weight, such as grains, pennyweights, ounces, pounds, stones, hundredweights and tons. In 1965, Britain abandoned the

In British markets, fruit is still sold using the imperial system—the seedless grapes are being sold by pounds weight in this instance.

awkward imperial system in favour of the SI (Systéme International) metric units. Oddly enough, the only major country still using imperial units is not Britain—the originator of the system—but the United States. However, the use of imperial units in Britain lingers on, particularly in consumer oriented products, such as fruit, vegetables, meat, fish and milk. Thirty years after metrication, the local market in Britain still quotes its prices in decimal currency units per imperial weight measure.

Likewise, speed limits in Britain are quoted in miles per hour. Speedometers in British cars feature dials in both miles per hour and kilometres per hour.

Product Design and Quality Standards
The British Standards Institute (BSI) is the principal body in the country that establishes the standards for specification of goods and services provided in Britain. Historically, design standards

issued by BSI have been the basis for standards adopted by many countries, particularly those of the British Commonwealth. Alternative design rules of similar status are standards issued by equivalent bodies in the United States, Germany and Japan.

European standards have gradually become harmonised under the International Standards Office (ISO) based in Paris. While local variations exist in most countries to suit residual historical anomalies, such as the specification for electrical plugs and sockets, EU standards are generally preferred in product specifications. BSI and offices of national standards in Europe publishes the *ISO Catalogue,* which provides a list of EU standards. The European practice of designing to a common standard is one of the industrial strengths of the EU. Products that are standard to the whole of Europe are marked "CE" to indicate conformity to European standard practice.

In accordance with general EU practice, most major companies are accredited to the ISO 9000 series of quality standards. Companies not holding ISO 9000 accreditation are increasingly excluded from markets, particularly those involved with supplying components to other companies rather producing stand-alone end products. BSI operates a programme to help industry qualify to the ISO 9000 series of quality standards. Enhancing the quality of goods produced by British industry is a policy of the present and past British governments. The government actively supports accreditation to the ISO 9000 standards through its subsidisation of BSI.

Research and Development

Even before the Industrial Revolution, England developed a culture of innovation that other nations lacked. From the time the country developed the longbow and armour-piercing arrows in the 12th century, England's military technology was generally ahead of its rivals in Europe. In the 1500s and 1600s, the country's state-of-the-art shipbuilding industry gave the Royal Navy an edge over its enemies. To allow British sailing ships to roam far and wide, the British developed the main navigational aids of the era—the chronometer and the sextant.

The innovative spirit really came to the fore with the Industrial Revolution. British inventors produced a seemingly limitless range of new machines—the steam engine, spinning machines, weaving machines, the blast furnace and steam powered trains and ships, to name but a few. While this innovative culture has caught on in other countries, the tradition continues in Britain. By most measures, Britain remains the world's most innovative country.

The spirit of innovation appears to come, more than anything, from an innate culture of curiosity rather than any deliberate policy of the state. One of the factors could be the fact that British society tends to be highly individualistic rather than conformist. High academic standards in some schools might be another. At the tertiary level, the top universities in Britain have matchless traditions of excellence.

Curiously enough, the commercial climate in Britain does not favour the innovator. The government provides limited financial

---

Measures of British Inventiveness

According to Japan's Ministry of International Trade and Industry, 40% of the world's leading product discoveries of the past 50 years have been made in Britain.

On absolute terms of the number of Nobel Prizes won, Britain trails only the United States, which has four times the British population. On a per capita basis, Britain has won more Nobel Prizes than any other country.

Britain has a prodigious output of scientific ideas, ranking just behind the United States as the world's leader in the production of scientific papers. On the other hand, based on the sheer volume of patents lodged, the United States is way ahead of all other countries, with Britain trailing both Germany and Japan, sharing fourth place with France.

inducement to the development of new technology. Most of society's commercial and social kudos are granted to the giants of the financial and legal world.

None of this has affected the British inventor, however. Britain is one of the world's most individualistic societies, where battling adversity is considered a badge of honour. British inventiveness often stems from individual genius rather than corporate effort. People pursue their hobbies with passion. Foreign investors looking for new product ideas may find Britain a fertile hunting ground for unearthing impoverished geniuses with products of commercial potential. The British have also acquired a reputation for failing to commercialise their inventions. The image of the eccentric British inventor who beavers away by himself in his own laboratory is really quite true to life. A favourite British role model is of an absent-minded professor who dreams constantly of his breakthrough ideas but cannot be relied upon to tie his shoelaces when he wakes up in the morning.

Despite a prodigious output of ingenious inventions over the years, British technology is not highly regarded in the British community. Engineers and technicians are poorly paid and enjoy poor status, and scientists have fared even worse in recent times. New right philosophies that no project was worth doing unless it produced an immediate return on investment had good innings under the Conservatives, who made progress in the area of dismantling all fundamental scientific research on the grounds that it was a waste of money. Scientists, grudgingly employed on one-year contracts had problems obtaining funding for long-term research. These discouragements saw enrolment for science and technology drop over the years. Many of today's young intellectual giants seek to study law or economics, then head for the City where they can expect to pull in six-figure incomes.

So far as the foreign investor is concerned, the unfashionability of technology as a career option may be an advantage. Salaries and wages of professional engineers and tradespeople are considerably less in Britain than in places such as Germany and France. Arguably, you are likely to get more engineering talent for your money in Britain than most places.

In the 1980s and 1990s, Britain's expenditure on research and development (R&D), expressed as a percent of GDP, is about the EU average of just over 2% of GDP. However, over the same period, the proportion of GDP devoted to research and development by Germany, the United States and Japan was about

---

Famous British Inventors and their Inventions
Inventions, such as the Spinning Jenny, the steam engine, macadamised roadways, the railways and the telephone, were some of the inspirations of British inventors that underpinned the Industrial Revolution.

British inventors of the 20th century have been equally busy in perfecting breakthrough products, generally with little encouragement from either business or government. British inventors often convey the appearance of gifted amateurs. This is perhaps a large factor in their success. Britain today is the home of gentlemen scientists in the 18th and 19th century mould

Frank Whittle, who invented the jet engine, and John Logie Baird, who invented television, persevered despite the derision of colleagues of lesser talent. Other inventors were charged by the government to innovate products with specific applications. In 1943, during World War II, a team headed by British mathematician Alan Turing built Colossus I, the world's first electronic computer, to break the codes of the German High Command.

Connection with prestigious institutes of learning assisted some British inventors, who nevertheless conducted their research projects outside normal office hours. Gordon Dobson—a pioneer of atmospheric chemistry that later proved vital in studies of ozone layer depletion—completed his breakthrough work in his home laboratory while he was professor of geography at Oxford University. James Lovelock, who developed the Gaia hypothesis of the earth and its biosphere, worked almost entirely in isolation in a laboratory connected to his home in Cornwall.

25% higher than Britain's effort. But when it comes to R&D, mere money is unlikely to tell the full story. With its ongoing traditions of eccentric genius, Britain appears to get more for its research dollar than any other country.

The government offers limited direct financial encouragement to R&D. DTI operates a range of investment grant programmes partly aimed at encouraging innovative technologies (the other principal objective is to develop depressed areas of the economy, such as the old industrial cities of the Midlands). Expenditure on research and development attracts a modest tax concession—the full capital cost of R&D projects can be deducted against current year profits.

Intellectual Property

The protection of intellectual property that originated in Britain is covered by the Patent Office—DTI's subsidiary organisation. The Patent Office is linked to the controlling body for lodgement and approval of patents, the World Intellectual Property Office (WIPO) based in Geneva, Switzerland.

Patent laws are being simplified. Until recently, intellectual property had to be covered by patents taken out separately in every country in the world in which the product was to be made or marketed. Applying for separate patents for most of the countries in the world (each written in the language of the country in which the patent was being taken out) presented a costly challenge for people with new product ideas. As a result, development of new ideas was stifled and embarking on a product development programme was simply too daunting to all but the most persevering small time inventors.

A programme is presently underway to overcome this problem. Intellectual property legislation within the EU is being harmonised with the object of streamlining this area of law. Under the EU legislation, a single trademark or patent application and a single copyright will be valid for all EU countries. Inventors in the EU and their sponsoring companies will greatly benefit when this legislation takes effect. Cost and delays in the granting of patents will be greatly reduced and the geographical area of patent protection will be greatly increased. Improved patent and copyright laws that the harmonisation process produces will greatly benefit Britain's highly innovative culture, where new product ideas per capita are generated at a greater rate than most other countries.

Environment

Before humans set foot on the British Isles, most of the terrain was under forest cover. Over its long history of human settlement, the countryside has been gradually deforested. In today's Britain, 10% of the land area is set aside as forests and woodland, with 25% used for arable land and 46% used as permanent pasture.

Britain is an environmentally aware society. In response to a 1998 survey conducted by the Department of the Environment, 88% of respondents claimed to be concerned about the environment. The British have a particular affinity with their countryside and are at pains to keep it in good condition. In the 1997 election, although the Green party attracted over two million votes, this was not enough to win the party a seat in the House of Commons under Britain's "first past the post" electoral system.

Unspoilt areas are protected from development. The British government has legislated to keep in pristine condition 36 areas of outstanding natural beauty, six forests, 22 environ-mentally sensitive areas, 1,000 km of coastline, thousands of historic buildings and hundreds of nature reserves.

The physical environment in British cities has improved greatly since 16th century, when householders used to tip their garbage into the street, burn coal to heat their houses and dump their sewage into drains that discharged directly into streams. Air and water quality in cities has improved, as well as the physical appearance of the cities themselves. Over the last 10 or 15 years, most cities in Britain have run programmes to clean the facades of their buildings, removing grime deposited by decades of coal

The Rise and Fall of Fisons

In the early 1990s, Fisons plc was a highly profitable conglomerate, having been the subject of a spectacular turnaround during the 1980s. A 1986 poll conducted by stockbrokers James Capel rated Fisons the best managed company in its sector. Though the company was considered too secretive by some, it continued to be a darling of stock market analysts throughout the early 1990s.

Fisons had three profit centres—pharmaceuticals, scientific equipment and horticultural products. Of these, horticultural products was by far the smallest in terms of both turnover and profit. The major product of the horticultural division was peat obtained from various Yorkshire moors considered by conservationists to be environmentally sensitive areas. By the end of 1989, the company's operations on the moors had attracted the interest of organisations like Friends of the Earth, the Royal Society for Protection of Birds, and the Worldwide Fund for Nature. A photographer sent to the site by the investigative newspaper, *The Sunday Times*, had to be rescued by police after Fisons' employees detained him, demanding that he hand over the photographs that he had just taken of peat excavation activities.

Conservationists formed the Peatlands Campaign to oppose Fisons. Led by the Prince of Wales, the Peatlands Campaign urged gardeners to boycott peat products and thereby save the remaining peat bogs. The Peatlands Campaign contacted fund managers and pension funds, which owned about 40% of the company's stock, to pressure the company to curtail its peat business. The matter was also debated in both Houses of Parliament.

Instead of backing down and getting on with its pharmaceutical and scientific business, Fisons decided to fight the conservation issue—with disastrous results. By the end of 1995, the company was a shell of its former self. Three CEOs had arrived and departed in quick succession. By the end of 1996, the company was out of business and the corporate remnant was sold to a competing drug company.

The River Thames in London has been cleaned up considerably since the 19th century, when it was used as a dumping ground for garbage and waste matter.

burning. The River Thames in London has been cleaned up so successfully that it once again supports a thriving fish population.

The country is still making progress on cleaning up heavily polluted estuaries, in particular the Forth, the Tees, the Thames and the Tyne. Air quality of most cities has improved, with London receiving 70% more winter sunshine hours than the "smog" days of the 1950s.

The controlling legislation relating to the environment is the Environmental Protection Act (1990), which applies to England, Scotland and Wales (but not Northern Ireland). This act encompasses a wide range of environmental interests, including control of liquid and solid waste, air and water pollution, disposal of garbage, control of litter and provisions for noise abatement.

Other government bodies, such as the National Rivers Authority (NRA), are responsible for specific aspects of the

The Thames Barrier
The water level of eastern Britain is rising as a result of global warming. The ground level of the eastern seaboard is sinking, continuing a process that created the North Sea. In fact, much of the capital of London now lies below the level of the high spring tide. Over the years, embankments on London's River Thames have been raised progressively to protect the city from high water levels that occur when high tides coincide with storms. A removable barrier has been built east of the city at Woolwich to provide additional protection against storm surges sweeping up the Thames from the east

environment. The government recognises that the various aspects of environmental control, such as the health of rivers and the disposal of liquid waste, interact with and impinge on each other. The number of independent environmental protection bodies is gradually being whittled down and their responsibilities absorbed by the Department of the Environment.

On the international scene, Britain took a prominent pro-environmental role in the Kyoto Conference on controlling greenhouse gas emissions in December 1997. It was also one of the first signatories to the 1987 Montreal Conference to control the release to the atmosphere of ozone-destroying CFCs and halons.

However, Scandinavian countries have complained that sulphur dioxide released from British coal burning power stations have generated acid rain, which has damaged their pine forests and acidified their lakes. Britain has responded to these complaints by imposing more stringent emission standards on power station operators. There has been a shift away from coal power generators to cleaner gas fired generators. As a result, sulphur dioxide emissions has been halved over the period from 1975 to 1996.

> **Nineteenth Century Report: Foul Waters of the Thames Brings the Nation to a Halt**
>
> The Houses of Parliament were constructed on the Thames in 1840. At that time, the Thames was used as an open sewer by communities living alongside the 200-mile river. When the Thames and its load of waste matter reached the nation's capital, it was rank, particularly during summer. The fragrance of "eau de Thames" would drift across the Embankment on the prevailing south-westerly breeze and make its way into the House. On several occasions during the 19th century, honourable gentlemen of the Chambers were forced to retire to their country estates until a change of wind direction allowed them to resume the task of administering the nation.

Environmental Design Standards

ISO 14001 is the standard that prescribes the environmental design rules relating to products. Compliance with this standard is presently voluntary but in the future, it will likely become mandatory for more and more industries. Products that comply with environmental design standards will have a real edge in the marketplace. Successful chain stores, such as The Body Shop, were founded on the notion that environmentally aware consumers are a powerful force in the market. In recent years, competitive shops, such as Boots—Britain's largest pharmaceutical chain—has also adopted green marketing strategies, leading to a decline of the market leadership of The Body Shop.

The EU has developed an "ecolabelling" scheme for consumer products. At present, company participation in this scheme is entirely voluntary. The objective of the scheme is to provide information for consumers who are influenced by environmental considerations. A similar voluntary scheme for "energy" ratings measures the energy efficiency of the products being offered.

> **Green Marketing**
> In a 1992 survey, 53% of consumers stated they had not bought
> certain products in the previous year because they were concerned
> about the effect of the products on the environment.
>
> Supermarket chain Tesco reacted to the findings by running
> an advertising campaign announcing that products sold in its stores
> were environmentally safe. Car rental group Avis decided to fit
> catalytic converters to its fleet of cars and concentrated its
> advertising on its "green" image. Following the same idea, Hertz
> installed a "tidy bag" in its cars to discourage littering.
>
> In a long running campaign that attracted extraordinary
> publicity over a very long time, three private individuals took US
> fast food company McDonald's through the appeal court of
> England over various environmental issues. The case was in the
> news continuously as a David versus Goliath story that, in this
> instance, was eventually won by Goliath. Though McDonald's
> won the legal case, the publicity was damaging and environmental
> consciousness was boosted.

Under both schemes, adhesive labels rating the environmental
and energy performance of the model being offered are issued to
manufacturers to affix to their products. Favourable energy and
environmental ratings may help sell the product to environmentally
aware consumers. Interested parties of this scheme can obtain
further details from the Department of the Environment.

Pollution Control
British legislation to protect the environment is fairly strict and
likely to become more so. Businesses establishing operations in
Britain should be careful not to infringe anti-pollution regulations.

Within England, the body responsible for ensuring that
industry meets environmental guidelines is the Environmental
Authority for England and Wales (EA). Equivalent regional bodies
exist for Scotland and Northern Ireland. The responsibility of
implementing pollution measures falls to either local authorities
or the EA, depending on the nature of the pollutant. Businesses

producing only routine solid and liquid waste will fall within the powers of the local authority.

Solid wastes are mostly disposed of by land filling, with little recycling. This is likely to change in the next five to ten years as the government imposes more stringent regulations on land filling and incineration. In addition, a landfill tax was introduced in 1996 to serve as an incentive to minimise waste. This tax will likely be passed on to the investor by waste disposal contractors.

Generally speaking, an investor setting up a "run of the mill" business need not become intimately familiar with the environmental laws in regard to disposal of waste products. A minor industry of waste subcontractors exists in Britain to remove most noxious wastes for a fee. These people will remove the waste from your premises and take care of it according to the rules and regulations of the EA. At the same time, the EU is in the process of implementing the regulation that a minimum of 50% of solid waste be recycled. The waste contractor may then require that clients pre-sort waste into categories, such as paper, plastic and metals.

Liquid and airborne effluents are generally less tractable than solid waste. Small amounts of noxious liquid waste, such as used machine oil may be collected by liquid waste treatment contractors and taken off the premises to be treated in an approved manner.

Where the process of production produces significant quantities of liquid waste, however, storage of liquid waste for collection and disposal by others will not be practicable. Such waste must then be treated in a manner approved by the EA, which will involve obtaining consent from the EA for the treated liquid or airborne effluent being discharged.

Summary
Trading on both import and export accounts is increasing as a percentage of GNP. Tariff regulations are the same as other EU countries. British business people normally formalise agreements between contracting parties in legal documents. In the event that

you have to write a legal document or you want someone else's legal document reviewed, you will need the services of a solicitor. If you do not already know a solicitor, take care in selecting one for the first time. A trusted solicitor that you can get along with can be a valuable silent partner to your business. On the other hand, stories of unsatisfactory dealings between clients and their solicitors are commonplace. Employment regulations in Britain are far from onerous. Nevertheless, the regulations do impose some obligations on employers. The culture of intellectualism and inventiveness that has been a trademark of British history is still alive and well. Britain is a fertile breeding ground for innovative individuals. Like most of the EU countries, Britain is becoming increasingly environmentally conscious—a circumstance that both presents opportunities for businesses selling environmentally friendly products and imposes certain costs for dealing with the waste products of the industrial process.

CHAPTER 7

Culture and Customs

Cultural Origins

The majority of people in Britain are Anglo-Saxon, a race which, according to its detractors, lives in a permanent state of emotional self-control. The English "stiff upper lip"—indicating calmness in the face of difficulty—is a somewhat self-deprecating figure of speech to describe this characteristic.

To regard Britain as an Anglo-Saxon nation, however, is to oversimplify the racial mix. Britain is a polyglot society—the Anglo-Saxon model is by no means universal. Over the centuries, races from most of Europe and much of the rest of the world have arrived and settled in various localities that now enjoy distinct subcultures. Dialects and customs vary quite markedly from one part of the country to the next.

There are also many regional divisions in Britain, where behaviour and speech patterns can vary greatly between communities that are only a small distance apart. Some stereotypes follow. People from Yorkshire are generally thought to be direct and taciturn, whereas the Welsh are indirect and voluble. The Scots, the Irish and the Cockneys may be highly sociable, with their societies often centred around the local pub. West Country English are hospitable but speak with a burr that can be difficult to penetrate. As an additional ingredient to the racial mix, a large number of recently arrived minority ethnic groups have imported much of their indigenous culture. These people are spread over the country but concentrate in cities.

Contrasts between rural and urban communities are also rather marked. Should you walk down a country lane and pass a local stranger coming in the opposite direction, you will, more often than not, receive a "Good morning" or a "Good evening". On the other hand, you will unlikely get such a greeting when you brush past someone in the streets of a town.

Overlaying the regional variations of different groups is class distinction, lingering from British history and perpetuated by inherited privilege. Aristocrats are great practitioners of dispassionate Englishness. The upper class accent, popularised in Victorian times, is the mark of this segment of British society. Conversational style is detached but unfailingly amusing. In its most extreme version, personal views are delivered entirely in the third person, with opinions starting with the pronoun "one". This construction is used in particular when describing something distasteful—something from which one wishes to dissociate oneself.

Onepersonship

Prime Minister Margaret Thatcher was a great user of the third person construction in the speeches she delivered when in office (in contrast to Winston Churchill, who was considered the finest speechmaker in British history and has more entries in *Quotable Quotes* than any other single individual).

The ultimate accolade in dismissing the distasteful belongs to Queen Victoria, who, in a memorable line, displayed her contempt for an attempt at light-heartedness at her expense. "We are not amused", declared the queen, referring to her own personal reaction rather than that of the monarchical collective.

Fifty years ago, there were three distinct classes: the upper class at the top, the working class at the bottom and the middle class in between—represented by bank managers and the like. Vestiges of working class deference to the ruling classes still remain. Cab drivers may still address you as "Guv'nor" and perhaps tug at his forelock in a faintly derisory manner. The paper seller in the newsstand may do likewise when he hands you the change for your paper.

The British enjoy a self-effacing sense of humour, much of which springs from the interaction between the various social and racial groups in British society. This is a trait that shows up in many British movies and television series—for example, *Coronation Street, Eastenders* and *Yes, Minister*.

Personal Space

The British may be gregarious but they also value privacy. They like to have a place within themselves to which they can retreat for a while. Anglo-Saxons enjoy the feel of *space* around them. A good working rule is to leave two feet between you and your conversational partner—except where environmental conditions make this distance impracticable, such as commuting inside crowded tube trains.

Since the English tend to keep their distance, they are not known to be "touchers". The principal gesture between men is the handshake, used on meeting, greeting, departing and betting. Women are a little less inhibited. They may kiss, embrace, shake hands or merely wave at each other from within their personal space—depending on how they feel. Men and women who are not intimately involved with each other may shake hands or kiss each other on the cheek, according to the strength of the relationship.

Non-verbal gestures are fairly standard. Of the facial gestures, raised eyebrows indicate surprise, nodding indicates agreement and shaking the head indicates disagreement. Thumbs up means agreement, thumbs down means failure and a single upward finger gesture is a very rude sign. Below the waist body language is fairly liberal. Crossing the legs is acceptable. No particular angle of the feet is prescribed, but it is not a good idea to display the soles of the feet to people of minority ethnic groups, such as Arabs and East Asians, who might follow their own minority customs. Putting the feet up on the desktop is also not recommended.

On meeting someone for the first time or if you are talking to them, you are meant to establish some eye contract but not to the point of staring down the other party, which would be intimidatory and rude. As in most cultures, it pays to smile when the opportunity arises, but once again, not to the extent of wearing a permanent fixed smile, which would be considered as odd, false or worse. Of high profile people in British life, businessman Richard Branson is a person who smiles consistently and for long periods. Prime Minister Tony Blair is another.

Character Types

British television comedies and films usually draw much of their humour by playing on the interaction between the various stereotypical British character types, of which there are many. The serial *Steptoe and Son* displays the mores of Cockneys in a small business. Nothing could be further from this than the aristocratic tones heard in the city a few miles west. The stereotypical Yorkshireman from north eastern England has a reputation for "calling a spade a spade" rather than an agricultural implement. In contrast, the aristocratic types who customarily inhabit the foreign office and immerse themselves in delicate international negotiations, are famed for their tact and diplomacy. In the west, the Welsh have a reputation for volubility and indirectness, whereas their counterparts in East Anglia are thought to be taciturn and to the point. The Irish are considered outgoing but argumentative, particularly amongst themselves. Some traits are associated with particular groups—for example, Scots are said to be "canny", in reference to their meanness with money (whether justified or not).

And so it goes. The British are a mixed race that has managed to preserve its tribal identities despite the homogenising influences of a mobile society, a common language and a small country. Overlaying the natural tribal divisions are recent waves of immigrants, traditional regional variations, a vast gulf between the socioeconomically advantaged and disadvantaged, aristocracy and inherited privilege and a lingering class system that traditionally divides the population into upper class, middle class and lower class.

With so many character types to identify, any general statements about the British consumer must be speculative.

Dogs, Cats and Other Pets

The British have an ambivalent attitude to animals. On the one hand, Britain is mostly a non-vegetarian culture. On the other, the British are genuinely fond of other species. As part of their commitment to the countryside and its inhabitants, Britons are avid members of societies that seek to advance the rights of wildlife

In a little known elevated corner of Edinburgh Castle sits the "Cemetery for Soldier's Dogs", where beloved pets of sentimental soldiers are buried.

such as birds, voles and badgers. They mount protests against animal experiments, raid chicken farms and challenge the aristocracy's rights to hunt foxes. They even throw acid at the fur coats of the rich and famous.

Many British people hang bird boxes from trees in their gardens and in winter, replenish the food tray each day. Avid bird lovers make detailed notes of the comings and goings of domestic birds, such as finches, tits, blackbirds, thrushes and so forth.

Then there is the great annual cuckoo competition. The cuckoo migrates south every winter and returns to Britain to breed. The cuckoo is undoubtedly Britain's most anti-social bird. It lays its eggs in the nests of other species then abandons its parental responsibilities to some long suffering bird half its size, which raises an ever hungry interloper whose first action is to kick all the genuine chicks out of the nest. With their inclination to sentimentality, it is surprising that the British place any store on the lifestyle of the cuckoo. However, the call of the cuckoo is very distinctive and is thought to herald the arrival of spring. Every year, there is an unofficial competition to be the one to hear the first cuckoo call of the season and have your letter published in *The Times*. To get one's letter published takes impeccable timing—after all, if the letter is sent too early, no one will believe it, including the editor of *The Times* letter page, and if sent too late, someone else will have got in first.

The British have possibly the world's highest rates of dog and cat ownership. Being a dog or a cat in a British home is as good as being part of the family—sometimes better. Most British pets are pampered and almost have the run of the house. When invited to a Briton's house for dinner, you will most likely receive introductions to various animals that also share the house, as well as be invited to view the birdhouse hanging from the bush in the back garden.

Religion

Britain is tolerant to all religions. Your religion will normally not be a barrier to doing business. In fact, it goes further. Under British law, discriminating against anyone on the grounds of a religious belief is an offence.

The principal religion in Britain is Christianity. Other significant religions include Islam, Hinduism, Buddhism and others imported from former British colonies in the Indian subcontinent, the Middle East or the Far East.

The principal Christian sect, the Church of England—otherwise know as the Anglican Church—is another early English innovation. The Anglican Church was founded in the 15th century by King Henry VIII after he was denied papal dispensation to divorce his wife and marry a young girl who took his fancy. To overcome this problem, Henry VIII renounced the Catholic Church and formed a church of his own, appointing himself its supreme head, a hereditary title currently held by Queen Elizabeth II.

York Minster is one of the largest medieval cathedrals in Europe, famous for its beautiful stained glass windows. The present cathedral was built between 1220 and 1480 and is currently undergoing restoration works.

Henry was hardly a godlike man. In his capacity as head of his new church, Henry married six women at various times, divorced three of them and murdered two. He robbed the monasteries, presided over a regime based on torture and duress and generally broke most of the Lord's commandments on a regular basis. In 1547, Henry died, probably of venereal disease, a common ailment in Europe at the time and variously known in England as "French pox", in France as "Spanish pox" and in Spain as "English pox".

At the 1990 census, 65% of Britons professed to believe in the afterlife. This has, however, not translated into church attendance. Congregations have dwindled in recent years. Nevertheless, as an owner of a great deal of property, the Church of England maintains its influence as an important business entity. The revenues of the church do not depend primarily on offerings in the collection plate.

Food, Booze and the British Public House

Traditional British

The British have been the butt of many a French joke for the blandness of their food. The traditional image is of a dish of meat and boiled vegetables with a total absence of flavour. Perhaps this is an exaggeration, but it has to be said, when endeavouring to describe British food, no particularly exciting, peculiarly British dish springs to mind. According to a recent survey conducted by the author, the most popular response to the question "What is the traditional English dish?" was "roast beef and Yorkshire pudding", followed by "fish and chips". Other contenders were "ploughman's lunch" (a roll with salad, cheese and pickle), cold pork pie and vindaloo curry. In the same survey, the traditional Scottish dish was returned as "haggis", the traditional Irish dish was listed as "potatoes" and the traditional Welsh dish was a mystery to almost everyone, with "seaweed soup" the sole suggestion.

Perhaps the alleged superiority of French cooking is partly semantics. After all, French dishes like *escargot de buerre* do conjure up more exciting culinary images than "snails in butter". Dishes that sound French are popular in England. Cooking is the area in which use of the French language lingers. There are always opportunities in Britain for continental restaurateurs.

Whatever the taste of their food, the British have a tradition for healthy appetites. Members of the 19th century British upper class were stern trencherpersons. The sentiment of the age was that since one needed money to eat copiously, obesity indicated wealth and was therefore socially desirable. The culinary day started at breakfast time with eggs, rashers of bacon, tea and toast. Hardly were the plates cleared away when at eleven in the morning, "elevenses" of tea and cakes would be taken. Then it was on to a multi-course lunch—soup, entrée, main course and sweets were the bare minimum. Tea was taken at about four in the afternoon, followed by a multi-course dinner that went on all evening.

Present-day Cuisine

Vestiges of these traditional eating habits remain. Although many British still eat a substantial breakfast, there has been a switch in recent years away from bacon and eggs to cereals. Elevenses is still widely practised. Lunch has become lighter, sometimes consisting only of sandwiches. Although business lunches may span the full gamut of courses, sandwiches are becoming more commonplace in the boardroom. For most people, dinner, consumed in the evening, is the main meal of the day.

Nutrition levels in present-day Britain are high and a wide range of foodstuffs is available. In the decade from 1986 to 1996, eating patterns moved noticeably from animal-based to vegetable-based products. Consumption of red meat and dairy products decreased, whereas consumption of fruit and nuts increased. Most conspicuous was a drop of 40% in the consumption of eggs and an increase of 25% of cereal products. The other major shift in eating habits has been from fresh to processed food and an increased consumption of pre-cooked takeaway food. Fast food is still a growing market in Britain.

Tastes have widened considerably, as more exotic foods and ingredients become available. Thirty years ago, *takeaway* conjured up visions of Chinese food and pizzas. The ethnicity of food on offer has expanded enormously. Migrants from countries, such as India, have entered both the fast food and restaurant businesses in a big way. Thais, Lebanese, Greeks and Turks have followed suit.

Elevenses and formal tea in the afternoon are less common than they were. Instead, cups of tea (or coffee) tend to be taken throughout the day. On a per capita basis, the British are still the world's number one drinkers of tea. From the historical perspective, the British attachment to tea was a very important factor in the development of their empire. The East India Company developed

Espresso cafés are springing up everywhere in London, as coffee threatens to overtake tea as the Britons' favorite beverage.

a monopoly in the tea trade. It was Parliament's attempt to maintain this monopoly that led to the Boston Tea Party and ultimately, the loss of the American colonies.

Despite a popular view to the contrary, coffee was the first of the two imported beverages onto the scene. Tea is said to have made its first English appearance in Garway's Coffee House in London in 1657. The contest between tea and coffee is still being waged today.

Alcoholic Drinks
Beer is Britain's most popular alcoholic drink. Traditional British beers are varieties of *bitter* consumed at room temperature. There has been a long-term shift to chilled lager beer, which accounts for about 50% of total beer sales today. Wine consumption has steadily increased. Although almost all wine is imported, at the end of 1997, there were 410 vineyards in the warmer parts of Britain producing mainly white wine. These are mostly small concerns. Home-grown wines have yet to make much impact on the British wine market.

The Pub
Much British social life is conducted inside a British pub (an abbreviation for *public house*). Pubs can be found throughout the

country—from the smallest villages to the largest cities. Most rural pubs are the village inns of hundreds of years ago. They are the social centres of the local communities, crammed with the bric-a-brac accumulated over their long histories. They have a homely atmosphere and, to many British, the pub is their home away from home and the publican is their best friend. Local publicans become part of the extended family of their patrons. Publicans have their fingers on the pulse of local commercial life so if you are seeking information about a locality, the local pub is an excellent research site. Publicans are normally happy to pass on whatever information they have to help the cause, particularly if you time your visit at one of the quiet times of the day when the publican will have the time to talk to you. Most pubs serve lunch and some serve evening meals, sometimes in a separate dining area, though more usually in a table inside the bar area. Pubs have a friendly atmosphere and are suitable venues for the informal entertaining or a quick business lunch.

Smoking

Medical statistics show that cigarette-related diseases led to 20% of all deaths in Britain. Surveys indicate that 69% of smokers claim they want to kick the habit. Fewer people are smoking than in the past, with 1997 statistics measuring the number of male smokers at 29% and female smokers at 28% of their respective population. The comparative figures for 1972 were 52% and 41%.

The economic burden on the community of treating the effects of cigarette smoking is about three times the amount raised in tobacco excise duty. The government will save money in the long run if it can engineer a reduction in smoking. However, it has limited means to implement this policy other than to legislate against tobacco advertising.

The Press

Britain is fortunate in having a large number of daily newspapers reporting the news from a range of viewpoints. Journalistic styles vary widely from the sensationalist "tabloid press" to sober and responsible broadsheets. There is an almost total lack of censorship. Within the limits of the country's very liberal libel laws, people can say what they like about each other—and they frequently do. Low circulation satirical papers, such as *Private Eye*, specialise in poking fun at establishment figures and stuffy institutions.

Like most countries, British papers are under competition from other news delivery systems—free-to-air and cable television, radio and latterly, the Internet. So far, the British have remained avid readers of newspapers. Sixty percent of people over the age 15 read at least one daily newspaper and 65% read a Sunday paper. It is not unusual for individuals to buy two, three or even four newspapers each day. Most of the main papers have survived, though there are occasional casualties. Like most places in the world, the number of evening papers has declined as people obtain their evening news through different media, principally television.

The Financial Times is the specialist daily for business. It contains a comprehensive update of financial information, including stock prices, exchange rates, value of unit trust and so on. It also carries a full range of articles on the economy, as well as more general news on politics and the general community.

Papers such as *The Times, The Daily Telegraph, The Manchester Guardian* and *The Independent* are considered highbrow daily papers. They contain comprehensive business sections. Middle of the road papers are *The Express* and *The Daily Mail*. These papers also include substantial business coverage.

The top selling newspapers in Britain are the "popular" tabloid dailies, containing plenty of pictures sparingly interspersed with columns of text. This segment of the media industry is declaimed by its detractors as the "gutter press". As a famous newspaper editor once remarked, "It is bad business to overestimate public taste".

Consistent with this philosophy, the "gutter press" outsells the quality broadsheets by a handy margin.

The Sun and *The News of the World* each sell about 4 million copies—the highest circulations in the country for daily and Sunday papers respectively. *The Sun* is a daily London paper best known for its page three photograph of a naked woman, with no particular connection to the news. *The News of the World* is a Sunday paper specialising in exposing the private lives of the rich and famous.

Both *The Sun* and *The News of the World* are owned by News Corporation headed by Rupert Murdoch, the international media mogul. Interestingly enough, News Corporation also owns *The Times*, London's most prestigious newspaper.

Photos of semi-naked people adorn the pages of the other "gutter press", with nakedness of the British aristocracy particularly valued. Photos of royal family flesh are at an absolute premium. The paparazzi, a particular brand of photographers making a living from this specialist industry, regularly expose themselves to great personal risk to ply their trade. They are sometimes shaken out of trees by royal bodyguards or even public-spirited citizens. Nonetheless, their pursuit of royal indiscretions can pay big dividends. In 1996, a German photographer managed to sneak an image of a naked Prince Charles through a crack in the curtains of a hotel room. The photo had a market value of over half a million dollars.

As well as the daily press, Britain has some first class weekly publications on business and the economy. *The Economist* is probably the pick of these, with *Financial Weekly* and *Investor's Chronicle* providing similar cover.

Unlike some countries in Europe, British newspapers are not subsidised by public money or political subscription. The British press says what it thinks, with some papers aligned to particular political parties and others neutral and still others switching from one side to the other. At election time, the editorial columns of most of the papers make a voting recommendation to their readers.

Editorial Policy

The political stance taken by papers may change from time to time at the whim of the proprietor. The most notable case in recent times was the switch of political support by the *The Sun*, which had traditionally supported the Conservatives.

In 1997, *The Sun* made the switch to Labour just in time to see Tony Blair to win the election, then claimed it had "caused" the election result. Cynics question what arrangement *The Sun* might have entered into with the Labour party. In any case, at the time *The Sun* predicted a Labour win, the result, according to rival papers and opinion polls, was a foregone conclusion.

Television and Radio

Technological advances in a number of areas have greatly increased the potential scope of radio and television broadcasting. The use of satellites increases the geographical coverage of line of sight transmission. The switch from analogue to digital signal offers the opportunity to transmit much more data and offers the possibility of interactive broadcasting for the first time. The potential of the new technologies has yet to be realised, indicating that the industry will continue to develop into the future.

At present, Britain has five free-to-air television stations that cover the entire country with basically the same format, although there are regional programmes in some areas. Two of the stations are government-run, courtesy of the British Broadcasting Commission (BBC), and financed by licence fees. The other three are commercial channels funded by advertising revenue. In addition, a number of satellite and cable television channels, funded by subscription income, account for 11% of viewing time. There is also a range of special services—for example, teletext service that broadcasts information, such as stock exchange prices, displayed as "pages" of text controlled by the user.

There are about 20 radio stations operating in Britain, most of which transmit to local districts. The BBC operates five national networks broadcasting a mixture of programmes. In addition, there are three commercial networks covering the country.

Sport and Other Recreational Pursuits

True to their innovative spirit, the British invented about half the world's most widely played competitive sports—golf, cricket, soccer, rugby, tennis and squash.

Invented in about 1860, soccer originated as a working man's game. It is now the world's most watched sport. In Britain, soccer still has a working class image, with rugby preferred in British public schools.

In 1997, nearly 80% of the population over the age of 16 years claimed to undertake regular physical activity. Sport—whether watching it or participating—has largely replaced religion as Sunday's main recreational activity. The camera lens has made sport into big business. If there is a limit to the public's interest in sport, it has yet to be reached. Increasing numbers of hours of sport are screened on television every year and a similar level of interest has flowed into other media. The proportion of papers devoted to sports coverage also increases every year.

Participant Sport and Recreation

Many British manage to blend their recreational interests with their love affair with the natural world. National surveys list walking as the most popular participant sport, with the largest number of participants, followed by swimming, snooker and "keep fit" activities. Other sports, such as village cricket, tennis and badminton, are widespread. The country has many golf courses. Darts is a national sport played largely in pubs. A few years ago,

Beach activities are a favorite recreational pursuit of the British. One of the most beautiful and popular beach resorts in England is St. Ives. Locals and tourists alike crowd its beaches during the summer.

the British marketed darts as a spectator sport and it became the most watched programme on television. However, television ratings of darts competitions have recently been in decline. The game has limited scope as an engrossing television spectacle.

Walking activities range from exercising the family dog to undertaking a journey by foot from Land's End, the south westernmost tip of Britain, to John O'Groats at the other end. Rural Britain is crisscrossed by about 4,000 km of walking tracks and the British take their walking seriously, with route maps, instructions for correct walking and survival techniques, and a list of courtesies that will preserve the walking infrastructure for others. Where registered tracks cross private land, landowners are obliged to maintain the condition of stiles and gates on behalf of the walking public. The network of walking trails is increasing. A new national trail following the route of Hadrian's Wall will be ready by 2001. Further trails are planned for the Cotswold Hills, the Pennines and areas in Wales and Scotland.

Aside from more formal sporting activities, national surveys list gardening as the most popular recreational pursuit. The "English country garden"—the subject of a popular song—is a national institution. Plant nurseries selling shrubs, flowers, seedlings, fertiliser and gardening equipment are a minor industry. Established horticultural exhibits, such as the Chelsea Flower Show and Kew Gardens, are major tourist attractions.

Sport and National Prestige

In some national sports, the British still retain the vestiges of amateurism and sportsmanship, where the idea lingers that the game may be played for its enjoyment, regardless of outcome. However, since the deeds of successful national sports teams imbue a sense of electoral wellbeing that transfers as votes for the ruling party, winning at the national level is becoming politically important. In the 1997 budget, the United Kingdom Sports Council set aside funding for developing elite sportsmen and women. The expressed purpose of this funding was to "produce a

---

Was Eddie the Eagle the Last of a Species?

Perhaps the last individual to pursue the Olympic ideal that the important thing is to participate rather than win was Eddie Edwards, the British ski jump competitor in the 1988 Winter Olympics at Calgary. "Eddie the Eagle", who appeared to fall rather than jump off the end of the jump ramp, finished the competition with an absolute stranglehold on the wooden spoon for this event. The Eagle's unabashed lack of soaring ability was the talk of the games and considered a true demonstration of the British belief in the spirit of amateurism.

A Night of Shame at Wembley
Since they won the World Cup in 1966, England's soccer team has been the game's perpetual underachievers. By and large, Scotland, Wales and Northern Ireland have fared even worse. The news that the English soccer team of full-time professionals has once again been humiliated at Wembley by a scratch team of amateurs from the Ruritanian second division is reported in the press as something akin to losing a minor war.

constant flow of world-class performers and winners" to joust for the country's honour in the sporting arenas of the world. Now and again, however, a few British sports people of appealing amateurism still make it to the top under their own steam

The fortunes of national sports teams, as distinct from individuals, are very important in the British psyche. Today, to the chagrin of the average British sports fan the rest of the world often beats the British at games it invented.

English cricket has gone through a 30-year slump, with the West Indian, Australian, Indian and Pakistani teams all successful against the home side. The real passion, however, is soccer, widely regarded to be more important than cricket. Britain, England, Wales, Scotland and Northern Ireland field separate national teams, whose fortunes the British follow very seriously. When the home team loses once again to a rank outsider, national statehood has been impugned and the papers report the result in those terms.

As in other cultures, business can be done while participating in sports of a leisurely nature. The most widely played business game is golf, which puts two or more parties together for a period of four or so hours of gentle exertion interspersed with frequent opportunities for conversation. Many gentlemen's clubs also provide facilities, such as squash and tennis courts, enabling business to be done over drinks following the game.

Sport as an Entertainment Business

Sport is one of the fastest growing attractions on television, with popular sports programmes earning top viewing ratings. Sports clubs, in particular soccer clubs, have established themselves as multi-million dollar business, with off-field sales of endorsed products and television royalties greatly exceeding gate takings.

Big money flowing into sporting clubs has translated into vast salaries to top players, who have become business inputs to be

Soccer club jerseys, scarfs, caps and other merchandise are sold in every street corner in Britain.

traded. Huge transfer fees are paid to lure proven performers from other clubs. Likewise, fabulous prize money is distributed to golf and tennis tournaments that used to be the province of amateurs 30 to 40 years ago.

Television has enabled sport to be viewed as never before, with close-ups of players and audio-visual sophistication that even attendance at the event cannot rival. The easiest way to view sports is in your own home.

> **Sport on Television**
> In September 1992, the satellite television broadcaster BSkyB launched Sky Sports channel, having secured exclusive rights to broadcast Premier League English soccer for five years. In less than six weeks, subscribers to BSkyB nearly doubled to 2.7 million. BSkyB then moved on to other sports, offering huge sums to sporting bodies for exclusive rights to one-day cricket, rugby union, international golf and rugby league—for which sport it formed its own Premier League involving regular competition between teams from the United Kingdom, Australia and South Africa. By September 1996, BSkyB's sports strategy had increased the number of subscribers to 3.6 million. It was providing 28 channels compared to five for terrestrial-based television and was easily the most profitable television station in Britain.

Crime

As in most of the world, crime in Britain is increasing, with offences reported to police rising by about 20% over the past 10 years. Criminologists blame increased crime statistics primarily on the increased use of drugs. Crime is very heavily regionalised, being concentrated in underprivileged urban areas. Burglary, theft and fraud are the biggest crimes statistically. Only 7% of reported crimes in Britain are crimes of violence. By and large, Britain is a country where an individual can walk about in reasonable safety without fear of attack. There are, however, some inner city urban areas that are better avoided.

Of all crimes in Britain, terrorist attacks attract the most media attention. Since the conflict started in Ireland and the Middle East, marginalised people have taken to expressing their political viewpoints by exploding bombs in public places, such as busy streets and department stores. The British are very conscious of these bomb threats. If you happen to be using a railway station and are looking for somewhere to deposit your rubbish, you may discover that no rubbish bins are within sight. You may also find that letter boxes have very narrow slots that admit only one letter at a time. Bins and letter boxes are regarded as natural repositories for bombs and have been either withdrawn from service or made bombproof. You will see signs everywhere and hear public announcements advising you not to leave your bag unattended. If you do, even for a short period, your bag will be taken away by the bomb disposal squad for disposal.

The police force in Britain, numbering about 120,000, is provided by local authorities and has a local touch. True to life is the television image of the friendly local "bobby" who will willingly provide tourist information about his beat.

The Royal Family
British pomp ceremony is not merely tradition. These days, it is big business and a British premier tourist attraction. At the epicentre is the royal family. With its adventures and misadventures, this family of fairly nondescript individuals is the world's single biggest ongoing media event, or as some would say, media circus. It has produced a sub-class of media personnel, the "royal watchers, who write articles and books on the royals, invade their private moments with camera lenses and phone taps, tail cars suspected of containing royal specimens and generally, make a living out of this one subject. Magazines, particularly women's magazines, provide a steady market for the output of these royal watchers.

Critics have pointed out that the cost of running the royal family is considerable. Royalists rallying to the cause point out the foreign exchange generated by tourists witnessing such royal events, such as the changing of the guard, far outweighs the running costs of the queen and her retinue. The royalists might well be right. The return on investment of the royal family has proved difficult to quantify. However, the fact is that the annual subsidy to the royal family from the public purse is only £8 million per year—small potatoes compared to their contribution to the economy of the tourist industry. The bulk of the royal income comes from its extensive property holdings.

Summary

The British are a mix of character types. The British society is a highly individualistic one—some might say idiosyncratic. It is an old society, sometimes steeped in its traditions, but often found at the leading edge, particularly in the development of technology. The old and new rest easily together. In more or less the same area, you will find the countryside perfectly preserved in its 16th century glory, with an ultra modern development just a few miles away. One of the engaging British traits is an ability to laugh at themselves, which they sometimes seem to do to excess. This trait underlies some of the very funny films and television series turned out by the British.

CHAPTER 8

Culture and Business

The Great Divide

The north and south of the country is not only divided by wealth but also by occupation. Merchant bankers are more likely to be found south of the divide and manufacturers north of it. The habits of the two types differ considerably. The north country tycoon is just as likely to be seen down the local pub quaffing a pint with his staff as he is to be found dining out with business associates. By and large, north country business people have a fearless reputation for gruffness and lack of subtlety, which they are often at pains to maintain when dealing with more polished colleagues from the south.

While there is some advantage in having connections and a public school education, no one who lacks these desirable credentials is excluded from a career in business, particularly if they come from places like Yorkshire or Lancashire. In fact, the English upper class has a fascination for those from the lower orders who achieve commercial success. Today, more than ever, British business people are drawn from all walks of life.

The Common Touch

Prime Minister Tony Blair, representing the northern electorate of Sedgefield, has been careful to maintain the common touch that helped him win his seat and the leadership of the Labour party. Harold Wilson, the prime minister 30 years before, had a similar style. Tony Blair was by no means born a common man. His father was a prosperous lawyer who could afford to send his son to Fettes Public School, Scotland's equivalent of Eton. From there, Blair attended Oxford University, studied law, was admitted to the bar and went on to Parliament.

The Conservative government developed a spirit of entrepreneurialism in Britain. At the end of the 1970s, Thatcher correctly recognised that many British were fed up with their welfare state and were ready to pursue a path that was more entrepreneurial, if less secure. Some of those who didn't necessarily share this world view had it forced on them anyway when they lost their nine-to-five jobs and had to strike out on their own.

Business Dealings

Many British people live a fairly structured life. More than most societies, the British are orderly creatures of habit. A British commuter will catch the same train to work each day, try to board the same carriage, expect to sit in the same seat (assuming all the other passengers in the train are of like mind, this is generally achievable) and settle back with the newspaper. Similarly, the commuter travels home on the same train each day and takes the family meal at pretty much the same time each day.

In this vein, the British are renowned as the world's greatest queuers. It is said that two Englishmen meeting in the street will instinctively fall in behind one another as a queue of two. People waiting for buses automatically line up to board the bus in the exact order in which they arrived at the bus stop. Unlike their unruly EU counterparts from Italy and Greece, the British miraculously merge into queues to present themselves in an orderly manner to bank tellers, information desks and airline check-in counters.

In the same way, British like their workday structured and orderly. They are not especially amenable to meeting people without appointments. Sales representatives who make a habit of walking in off the street may not get the best hearing—or any hearing at all. It is generally better to phone ahead and set up a meeting with someone in the company you wish to contact. The British are be punctual and reliable in making appointments. Arriving late does not make a good impression.

Meetings, like British life itself, tend to follow a set format. Attendees to a meeting arrive on time and stick to the agenda. Unlike other cultures, notably Asia, where people like to get to know you before they feel comfortable to discuss business with you, in Britain, you are more likely to get to know the people you are doing business with after the meeting is over—perhaps over a few drinks at a bar or at a dinner to celebrate the deal you have struck. From the British viewpoint, the purpose is to get things done rather than to socialise. Socialising may follow after the meeting is concluded. If you are dealing with a large company,

You Can Be Tested

Protocol in British life is hard to generalise. As a foreigner, you are unlikely to offend by sticking to your customary practices, provided they don't deviate too widely from local norms. However, if you are, for example, attending a job interview in Britain, you will be expected to – the traditional British way and exhibit appropriate behaviour.

A friend of the author relates the story of an interview he attended (he failed to get the job—or any other job—and wound up running his own very successful business making office chairs). On arrival at the interview, he was met by a secretary, told that the personnel manager was busy, offered a cup of tea that he accepted and shown to an anteroom furnished with two chairs, but no table. Moments after being handed his tea, the secretary and the personnel manager entered the anteroom and announced that the interview would commence and could the interviewee accompany them to the manager's office. Still holding his cup of tea, the hapless interviewee trailed into the manager's office and was seated on the other side of the personnel manager's desk, still holding his tea. There was nowhere to put the cup except on the personnel manager's desk, which he did. At that point, he knew he had blown the interview. The correct procedure, he realised too late, was to hand the tea back to the secretary in the anteroom. Then, he would have passed the first test of the interview—the niceties of protocol—and moved on to step two.

you may be required to have a preliminary meeting with a junior officer to explain your mission before you can get a meeting with the decision-maker.

Meetings are likely to be fairly polite affairs. There will probably be some small talk at the start of the meeting, but not too much. To kick things off, there may be some discussion about neutral topics, such as the weather or a traffic jam that has just ensnarled you. The senior member in the group will normally decide the length of the preliminaries. They will likely invite you to get down to business fairly soon, but not with such precipitate haste that overrides the niceties of protocol. The meeting agenda will be followed closely. Minutes will likely be taken and circulated to all participants. A conclusion will be reached and everyone will go about their business.

Familiarity versus Formality
In Britain 30 years ago, many people might have addressed their fellow participants at meetings by the respectful term "Mister" and equivalent female terms (assuming they did not have a superior title, such as "Sir" or "Archbishop"). Nowadays, address by first name is far more common, although the older practice of prefacing a title has not died out everywhere. The tone of the meeting will generally be evident from the way the other participants address each other. If the family name is used—as in "Jenkins, fetch the car"—you may be sure that the speaker is addressing an underling.

The natural inclination of the British is to compartmentalise their lives into business and private, with little overlap between the two. "Never mix business and pleasure" is an old adage of British business, indicating, in its ultimate expression, that business associates can never become personal friends. The theory is that personal issues may cloud business judgement if business and personal lives are intermingled. It is fair to say that few business people these days would go as far to interpose an impenetrable barrier between a business relationship and a friendship.

On first meeting, you may notice that your new British acquaintance is keeping his distance. Whether deservedly or not, the British are noted for their reserve, or as the French call it, their *sangfroid*. On the other hand, you may be able to turn the British reserve to your advantage by not being reserved yourself. Most British react positively to friendly gestures that put their relationships on a warmer footing. Simultaneous practice of *sangfroid* by both parties is not a practice recommended to advance the relationship. By the same token, crossing the line to over-familiarity could be considered offensive.

Business Dress Code

In the 1940s and 1950s, the British had reputations as dowdy dressers when compared to their stylish counterparts in Paris across the Channel. Sentiment changed in the "swinging" 1960s, however, with the emergence of the fashion houses of Carnaby Street and Kings Road in south-west London.

In British business, standard western dress code applies. Most men wear dark suits, plain or striped, with a shirt and a suitable tie. The trademark headgear for a British businessman, particularly those in the finance industries, used to be a bowler hat—preferably accompanied with a furled black umbrella. On a good day, you can still see a few bowlers around the City, but they are far less prolific than they once were. For businesswomen, a skirt or pant suit is the preferred apparel. The quality and cut of the material is important.

Foreign visitors who wish to wear the traditional formal attire of their originating cultures will not be considered out of place.

Eating Out and Other Entertainment

Lunch is an accepted way to entertain—particularly for new clients or prospects. If your lunch invitation is accepted, you are definitely making progress. No matter how promising the fare, the British will avoid lunching with someone whose company they don't enjoy. It is a good idea to book a suitable restaurant first. Naturally, as the person issuing the invitation, you will be expected to pay for the meal.

Dining in a restaurant is a much grander affair than lunch and not likely to occur directly after a first meeting. Whereas lunch would generally be between the people directly involved in the business, it is quite in order for spouses or partners to attend dinner parties. If you are invited to a club, this is likely to be an exclusive preserve for members only, where you have temporary privileges as an honoured guest.

After dinner, many forms of entertainment are available to suit a wide range of tastes.

London is a world centre for theatre, ballet and music. Other cities in Britain are also well provided with theatres in which touring theatre, dance and opera companies perform. Britain also produces a massive output of popular culture in films, documentaries, contemporary art and popular music. Various towns and villages around the country honour past literary figures with festivals. Buildings and areas in which these cultural icons lived and worked are also preserved and identified with them. For example, the area around Haworth in Yorkshire is "Bronte country". Similarly, one of the most visited villages in Britain is Stratford-upon-Avon, where William Shakespeare, the world's most famous playwright, lived.

Britain also stages various high profile sporting events throughout the year. The Wimbledon Tennis Finals and the FA Cup Final (soccer) head the list. International rugby and various horse races, such as the Derby at Ascot near London and the Grand National at Aintree in Lancashire, are also premier events. The prestige of the event is roughly proportional to the difficulty of obtaining tickets. If all else fails, tickets to sought-after sporting events and the theatre may be advertised in the press, particularly in *The Times* classifieds, usually at an extravagant premium on their face value.

London's West End is a centre for the arts and the theatre capital of the world, with world class musicals, plays and dance performed year round.

During the centuries over which British monarchs ruled the country, various rituals were established. These rituals endure, even though their underlying purpose may have vanished long ago. They are now tourist attractions that can serve as entertainment to visitors, provided there is the time and the inclination.

Opening of Parliament—The Tradition Lives On

An example of many British traditions constituting "pomp and ceremony" is the opening of Parliament, which has evolved from 700 years of tradition. It is now an annual television spectacular that is hard to match for entertainment value.

The evening before the next session of government, those responsible for guarding the Houses of Parliament, the Yeoman of the Guard, light candles and descend into the cellars of Westminster. They are re-enacting a search for Guy Fawkes, a disaffected Catholic who devised the Gunpowder Plot to blow up the Houses of Parliament and was burnt at the stake for his crimes in 1605.

On the day itself, a procession sets out from Buckingham Palace, comprising the Household Cavalry, mounted on black horses and armed with silver swords, and two gilded coaches, one containing the reigning monarch and the other containing the crown itself, travelling without human company.

The procession reaches the House of Lords, where the monarch dons the crown and enters the chamber to assume the throne. Since 1641, tradition decrees that no monarch may enter the House of Commons, so an intermediary is used at this point. The queen's messenger, known as Black Rod after the implement he carries, makes his way to the House of Commons. On arrival, he politely knocks on the front door (tapping the door with the end of his black rod). He is admitted to the Commons and passes on the queen's message that she is ready to open Parliament. The members of the House of Commons then make their way to the House of Lords. The queen then reads a speech, which is a summary of the government's political agenda for the coming parliamentary session.

The queen's calendar offers events open to the public. These are specifically British spectacles that overseas visitors can appreciate. Included are the Queens Gallery, inspection of the Royal Mews, Trooping of the Colour (a military exhibition for the queen's birthday on 13 June), royal garden parties (there are several per year) and the Royal Ascot Race Meeting (the third week in June). Tickets are sold at various times of the year. The number of tickets on issue is nowhere near the demand for them. They are usually sold out early. Ticketing details are available from Buckingham House publicity.

Other tourist attractions include the changing of the guard at Buckingham Palace and the Beefeaters at the Tower of London. Clad in pantaloons and funny hats and armed with military hardware developed in the 10th century, the Beefeaters maintain a 24-hour guard on the crown jewels inside the Tower.

Home Entertainment

In contrast to continental Europe where most people live in rented accommodation, about 70% of British people live in homes they own. Home and garden are absorbing interests of many British, and may well be major hobbies. When you drive around some of the older inner urban residential areas of established cities, you may be struck by the number of houses with scaffolded façades and a skip for containing rubbish at the front of the house. House renovation, with the objective of increasing property value, is an important investment avenue for many people. The home is not only seen as an abode but also an asset—perhaps the most important asset one will ever own. Renovation works may be completed by a professional builder, the property owner or a combination of the two. Britain has a "do it yourself" (DIY) culture and the DIY market is substantial, worth about £8 billion annually. By improving their properties, people can simultaneously increase their wealth, their comfort level and their social standing.

Making the most of a small space is the creator of this wonderful, whimsical balcony, decorated with colourful flowers—real and artificial—potted plants and windmills!

Instead of a restaurant, you may be invited to a meal at the home of your business associate. If this is someone you are trying to influence, you may count this invitation as a step forward. The British are selective about whom they invite into their homes. An old adage states, "The Englishman's home is his castle". For the British, therefore, the home is place of privacy into which its owner may withdraw to seek sanctuary from the outside world.

Your business associate may also have invited you to his or her home to impress you. People whose investment focus is their home like nothing more than to display the visible evidence of their success in life by inviting other people to admire the latest antiques they have acquired or the skills they have displayed in renovating the back room. Any compliments you make on the house, its contents, the garden or the skills of your host as a renovator can only add to whatever reservoir of goodwill you have already generated throughout your acquaintanceship.

Most likely, you will find your host and hostess doing the cooking themselves. Before World War II, the British upper and middle classes had live-in servants to take care of household chores, such as cleaning the house and cooking. Nowadays, this arrangement is most unusual. Britain has become a much more egalitarian society. Live-in help is found only in the homes of the ultra rich or those on lavish expense accounts, although occasionally the British may have outside caterers to help provide food for special functions.

At previous home hosted events, women did the cooking, while the men took charge of "masculine" activities, such as pouring the drinks and carving the joint (if there is one). With role reversal becoming more commonplace, however, this division of tasks between genders is by no means universal. For buffet-style affairs, guests may offer the occasional help with menial tasks, such as shuttling the food and beverages around the party. Your offer of help will likely be declined, but making the offer will be seen to be a polite gesture.

Bringing something to the dinner, such as a bottle of wine, is sometimes practised, but probably not appropriate in most cases. Other gestures, such as giving the host's children a small gift, is always appreciated.

Business Ethics

The British give the impression of being fairly scrupulous about their business dealings. Nonetheless, there is some latitude; indeed, some latitude is expected. There is really no limit to the amount of gift giving, particularly around Christmas, where, for good customers, a bottle of whiskey or even a case of wine, might be expected to accompany the Christmas card.

For occasions other than Christmas, gift giving is less common than it is in other cultures in Asia, for example. As such, your gift may be more appreciated and memorable. Novelty items, such as pens and pencils engraved with the name of your company, will always be acceptable and may even be treasured.

Appropriate gifts include consumables or low value durables. A case of whiskey, therefore could be interpreted as a gift (albeit a lavish one), whereas a television set of equivalent value might smack of bribery. The line is definitely drawn at cash payments of whatever amount. Where this line is drawn for durable gifts is a matter of judgement.

Business Cards

In times past, most business cards contained the full details of a person's qualifications. However, as more and more people obtain multiple and higher university degrees and other qualifications, such cards became cluttered with acronyms. The current practice today is to restrict the personal details on the card to name and job title.

The material presented on the card and the style of presentation varies with the industry. Cards of professionals, such as lawyers; titled people and high ranking executives comprise simple black text on a white background, conveying the image that the card holder thinks that as he or she is already a person with an established reputation, an eye-catching card with an elaborate display would be superfluous and perhaps distasteful. On the other end of the scale are real estate agents and sales representatives, whose cards may be multi-coloured, contain a photograph of themselves and maybe their products, and perhaps include some advertising material on the flip side of the card.

There are no standard dimensions to business cards. Most recipients of cards store them in cardholders suited to cards of about 70 mm by 45 mm—about the size of a credit card—with the text written along the longer axis. Cards larger than the standard size do not fit in standard size storage containers.

Computer-aided Presentations

Before, sales people would carry around catalogues of their products and sometimes, even a product sample if the product being sold was sufficiently portable. With the advent of notepad computers and the like, computer-aided presentations may be a more effective way to sell the product, particularly if computer animation software is included. The applicability of computer demonstration is to some extent governed by the product being presented. In this context, the author has participated in guided tours around magnificent houses (completely unaffordable) that were conducted without his leaving his office chair.

In the event that catalogue information is left behind, do not forget to include contact details of the product's distributor on the catalogue. In Britain, an extraordinary number of catalogues find their way into product libraries detached from their contact details—leaving a potential customer with the irritating problem of having found a catalogue description of the product he wants to buy but with no information regarding the source of supply.

Personnel Management

In the days that Britain was rigidly structured into upper, middle and lower classes, it was clear who gave orders and who took them. The class structure has weakened in the last generation but is by no means dead. At the extremities of the spectrum, people with bowler hats still issue orders to people in cloth caps. In this day and age, however, position in the pecking order for those in the middle is harder to determine.

Traditional British business practice was run on military lines with orders being passed up and down the hierarchy. This is not the favoured method for graduates of modern business schools where consensus management is recommended.

How you structure your new business in Britain is, of course, up to you. In some circumstances, you may have a structure imposed on you—for example, if you enter a business in Britain as a joint venture partner, the structure will most likely have been set.

The Nissan Plant

The British car industry has earned itself a well-deserved reputation for poor productivity and labour relations. The car industry grew around the cities of the West Midlands, where labour unions were strong. Over many years, foreign companies took over struggling British car companies and imposed their own corporate culture. By the end of the 1970s, the only car company left in public hands was British Leyland Motor Corporation (BLMC)—the remnants of Morris, Austin, Rover, Leyland trucks and various other British marques—which was reluctantly owned by the British government as a buyer of last resort. After forming an alliance with Japanese-owned Honda and being acquired by British Aerospace, BLMC (by then called Rover) was taken over by Bavarian Motor Works (BMW), the German manufacturer of luxury cars. The latest in a long list of owners, even BMW has not be able to fix the productivity and labour problems plaguing Rover's main plant at Longbridge in the West Midlands.

As a consequence of Rover's problems, the car industry in Britain attracted a lot of criticism. However, other manufacturers, imposing a different corporate culture to that inherited by BMW, have had quite a different experience.

When Japanese-owned Nissan Motors decided to set up a manufacturing plant in Britain, they took advantage of the government's development incentive scheme and located their plant in Sunderland, one of the most disadvantaged areas in Britain and one with very high unemployment rates. Nissan drew freely on the underemployed labour of the area and assembled a dedicated workforce willing to work within whatever terms Nissan chose to establish. Nissan employees were grateful to obtain a job at all and drew pride from the success of Nissan's enterprise. The Japanese work culture was established so successfully in this plant that it not only became the most productive car plant in Europe, but also became a model plant within the Nissan organisation for the training of workers from other plants, including those in Japan.

But if you are given a choice, modern management practices are generally more effective (these days, autocracies tend to perish more readily), where issues are discussed democratically before a decision is reached. In such management style, there will most likely be plenty of meetings at which all the people attending will want to have their say.

By and large, the British work well in an unstructured, free thinking environment. They have a tradition of producing eccentric yet brilliant, self-effacing inventors. They tend to be individualists who can work alone at finding ingenious solutions to tricky questions. They are temperamentally suited, for example, to the writing of software, of which they are Europe's leading producers.

If you start your own business in Britain, you will find that most British people are malleable and will, within reason, fit in with whatever the culture of the organisation happens to be.

Whether the British work in a foreign company or a local company is not normally an issue in employee relations. It is the business culture that the employer creates that is all-important. Some of the most successful companies in Britain are foreign-owned. British employees are more concerned about workplace issues than who owns the business. The British are more concerned about whether their jobs are secure, whether they have adequate resources to go to work, whether they clearly understand what they are meant to be doing and whether they take pride in their work and the organisation that employs them.

Education and Labour Skills

Legislation to make education compulsory was introduced in 1870. Subsequent education acts have raised the minimum school leaving age to 16 years. Literacy in Britain is about 99%.

The British secondary education system is a mixture of private and government-owned schools. Curiously, in Britain (and much to the bafflement of visitors to the country) the term "public" schools describes those that are privately owned.

Britain's oldest universities include Oxford and Cambridge University, which are regarded to be the best educational institutions in the world.

Government secondary education is provided through *comprehensive* and *selective* schools. Comprehensive schools admit all students to ensure that everyone gets the same educational opportunities. Critics see comprehensive education as institutionalising mediocrity, with educational standards being reduced to the level of the least able students. Selective schools, more commonly called grammar or secondary modern schools, admit students who have passed a proficiency test that they take at 11 years of age.

Prior to 1988, schooling was the responsibility of local government. The curriculum for each school was set by one of 104 local council education authorities, all acting independently. With the population more inclined to move in search of better job opportunities, this created difficulties for the increasing number of students who switched schools. In 1988, the government tried to standardise curricula and to raise the standards of the worst performing schools. In the same year, the Education Act was established, setting up a National Curriculum. By their nature,

British Education: A Curate's Egg

British education is a curious mixture. Across the population, Britain rates at the bottom of tables comparing international numeracy and literacy standards. On the other hand, elite British educational institutions produce more Nobel Prize winners per head of population than any other country. Top ranking British academics are at the top of other disciplines as well. For example, in 1988, British mathematicians snared two Fields Medals, the equivalent of the Nobel Prize in that discipline. In 1996, British mathematician Andrew Wiles, working out of Princeton, solved Fermat's Last Theorem, the most famous problem in mathematics and one that had defied the brains of the finest mathematicians for 358 years.

The highest British institutes of learning—Oxford and Cambridge University and Harrow and Eton schools—are regarded to be among the best in the world, if not the best. Cambridge University, which emphasises excellence in science and technology, was the institution at which Sir Isaac Newton—perhaps the greatest genius the world has ever seen—held the chair of mathematics and natural philosophy. It was at Cambridge that Newton conducted his famous experiments on light and wrote *Prinicipa Mathematica*, the textbook on the mechanics of the universe. In the 20th century, Cambridge University has produced Nobel laureates way out of proportion to its size (1997 enrolment was 13,500), amongst them Ernest Rutherford, James Chadwick and Paul Dirac in physics and Francis Crick and James Watson in biology, who unravelled the structure of the DNA molecule.

educational changes take a long time to evaluate. The results of the 1988 policy initiative have yet to be determined.

No comprehensive policy applies to public schools, which are privately owned. These schools set their own entry standards for selection of students. The standard of education offered by public schools is measurably higher than government schools and varies between one school and another. Public schools also offer social advantages later in life, as students establish a network of contacts with people who later gravitate to highly paid jobs, mostly in law, banking, and politics.

The parallel education system of public and comprehensive schools tends to perpetuate the classification of British society into privileged and underprivileged groups since only the well-off can afford public school fees. The offspring of the rich therefore start off their working life with an advantage.

In the last 20 years, the status of technical schools have been raised to that of universities, earning some resentment from the traditional universities and reducing the public perception of the value of a university degree. In the same period, the British economic ethic shifted from "support by the state" to "user pays". This ethic has now spread to almost all sectors of the economy, including education. Tertiary education is marketed in Britain as a product to be bought by the user rather than as an investment by the state in its people. The value of the education product has been under increasing scrutiny by its consumers. Recently, university enrolment have faltered as the job market for graduates diminished and people questioned the value of the degrees they were aspiring to acquire. University enrolment, which peaked in 1993, are presently in gentle decline.

The "open university" is an interesting British innovation in education. Students undertaking open university education complete their courses by correspondence, with tuition received through a combination of printed notes, television and radio broadcasts, video cassettes and the Internet. In 1997, there were 135,000 students enrolled for Open University first degrees and 15,000 enrolled for higher degrees.

Disadvantaged Areas

Most overseas interest in the United Kingdom is initially centred on London. But from a cost and convenience point of view, many of the other population centres in Britain are worth a look.

Wealth in Britain is unevenly distributed geographically. The reasons are historical. Towns and cities on which the Industrial Revolution was centred have lost much of the industry that once supported them. Some of them have found a replacement focus. Others haven't.

Cities in the south of the country that were always centres of trade, finance and commerce have prospered as these activities become the growth industries in the second half of the 20th century. The depressed areas are located in the midlands and north of England; in the main population centre of Scotland, along the west coast; and in southern Wales. Cities in Scotland and northern England have exhibited the classic symptoms of decline—a low level of wealth, unemployment, a high crime rate and urban decay. Such cities have had to cast off their past glories and find new roles for themselves.

Manchester, the first city of the Industrial Revolution, was a centre for textiles, an industry which still employed 384,000 people in 1998 through about 11,000 mostly small firms. Textile companies are under continuous threat from cheaper Asian producers, however, and the competitive situation will deteriorate further in 2005, when the Multi-fibre Agreement (MFA) that presently imposes restrictions on non-EU producers expires. In 1994, the textile firm, Coats Viyella, was amongst the 100 largest firms in Britain, but by 1998, it didn't rank in the top 350 firms.

Birmingham, Britain's second largest city, escaped the worst of the post-Industrial Revolution decline by becoming the centre of the new industries of the 20th century, in particular the car industry. However, under pressure from manufacturers in Asia and continental Europe, the British car industry entered a decline in the 1950s from which it has not yet recovered. The Rover plant at Longbridge in Birmingham, still the city's major industry, has been in a state of crisis since the late 1960s due to its inability to achieve productivity targets. The plant has been threatened with closure for a generation but is still in production.

Cities re-invent themselves on a regular basis, such as Glasgow, Scotland's largest city. Historically, the major industry of Glasgow was the shipbuilding industry along the river Clyde. Today, shipbuilding has moved offshore to places like Japan and Korea. Glasgow earned a reputation within Britain as a tough city decaying at the centre. The infamous Gorbals, Glasgow's inner urban slum, has been demolished and rebuilt twice—the first time as tenement blocks and the second time as low-rise housing. In the 1960s, most of the other cities also built tower blocks, which were later torn down after a generation of violence and property damage proved the failure of high-rise public accommodation as a social experiment.

Generally, the sense of urban decay is being removed from inner city areas, a programme which successive governments have actively encouraged through publicly funded rebuilding programmes. Under the EU urban renewal policies, depressed urban areas also qualify for concessional development. Towns and cities in the midlands and the north-east, such as Sheffield and Newcastle, were centres of the steel industry, which have recently reconstituted themselves as smaller high-tech units not centralised in any particular economic activity. No longer the city of William Blake's "dark satanic mills", Manchester has succeeded in re-inventing itself as a city of convention centres and new industry. Liverpool, once England's most important west coast port, fell into virtual disuse with the collapse of textile industries but is now experiencing a revival.

With their established infrastructure, investment incentives, lower costs for most services and a readily available pool of skilled labour, the provincial towns and cities of northern England and Scotland may offer advantages as a site for business activities of overseas investors intending to set up shop in Britain.

Summary

Modern day Britain offers an open, free enterprise economic environment in which minimum barriers are presented to business and the free exchange of ideas. The workforce is skilled, motivated and well-educated. The physical environment is fully developed. Business in Britain is respected as a noble tradition. Many of the trading houses of Britain can trace their origins back to the 16th century or earlier The markets of Europe are readily accessible. London has the advantage of being the centre of Europe's financial industry. After years of resisting physical invasion, today's Britain is completely open to outsiders. There are practically no barriers to foreign enterprise, foreign investment or repatriation of profits. A range of financial incentives is offered to encourage and assist business, particularly those establishing in depressed areas. Britain has a long history as a trading country. It likes to do business with the rest of the world

Basic Facts and Travel Tips

Climate

The prevailing wind is from the south-west, bringing ashore the weather systems of the Atlantic Ocean. A warm Atlantic current, the Gulf Stream, moderates the climate all-year-round. Winters are much milder than other countries on similar latitudes. Nevertheless, every winter, there are days of bitter winds and driving snow from the north and the east.

The mean maximum monthly temperature in London is 22°Centigrade in July and the mean minimum is 3°C in February. The hottest temperature ever recorded on mainland Britain was 37.1°C at Cheltenham in Gloucestershire on 3 August 1990 and the coldest was –27°C near Aberdeen in Scotland on 11 February 1895. There have been eight white Christmas days in London since 1900. The last occurred in 1981.

Britain is cloudy, particularly during winter. More than half the days in the year of days are overcast. Rainfall over the western half of the country is about double that of the east, with the wettest spot in the country being Styhead Tarn in northern Scotland, with an annual precipitation of 5000 mm. By comparison, the driest recording station in the country, St. Osyth in Essex, East Anglia, averages only 500 mm. Although rainfall is evenly spread through the seasons, recent climatic evidence suggests that Britain is becoming more Mediterranean, with drier summers and wetter winters. Another theory gathering support is that the melting of the northern ice cap due to global warming will shut down the Gulf Stream, thus turning the Yorkshire Dales into permafrost while most of the world heats up. Based on these two opposing viewpoints, all one can say at this stage is that British weather will continue to be unpredictable.

Weather Proofing—British Style

In building its infrastructure, the British never quite took into account their modest climatic extremes. Trains in the south-east are powered by an electrified ground rail that ices over during the few days of the year, when the temperature drops below freezing. The rail system chugs to a halt amidst declarations by the rail authorities of "exceptional weather conditions" (that occur almost every year). For the most part, southern England commuters accept their lot with stoicism, expecting nothing better than they got the previous winter.

Many buildings, too, withstand the climate poorly. Though double glazing has recently become more popular, much of British housing stock was constructed in the Victorian and Edwardian periods when poorly sealed sash windows were an architectural feature (about 90% of British windows remain single glazed).

In the few really hot days of summer, buildings can become uncomfortably hot since air conditioning, other than in office towers, is rare. Like New York, London can sometimes become quite muggy in summer, particularly in August.

Stately homes of a bygone era, though treasured by the British, tend to be leaky and poorly designed for conserving heat—drafty in winter and stuffy in summer.

Of course, not everyone can afford a stately home that once belonged to aristocracy. People of lesser means with a penchant to live in the past—and there are many—spend a fortune renovating and weatherproofing 15th and 16th century cottages that were built with few single horizontal and vertical surfaces. The houses were designed for peasants and stable hands who, judging from the height of doorways, must have been about five feet tall.

Documentation

Matters of Interest to Visitors

Health Regulations	No health certificate required
Visa Requirements	Varies with country of origin. Check with your local British consulate. No visas required for EU countries and North American countries.
Airport Tax	Departure tax of £20 (varies with destination)
Driving Licence	International licence is acceptable for up to 12 months. For people staying longer than 12 months, a local licence, requiring a driving test, must be produced.
Local Currency	Money laundering provisions. Currency exchange service is offered by most banks, in the post office and a by a large number of retail currency dealers.
Use of Credit Cards	All widely known cards can be used. Use of cards and electronic funds transfers is arguably more advanced in Britain than in any other country.

Electricity, Appliances and Computers

Voltage at point of use is 240 volt and 50 Hz. The British electricity distribution industry developed as separate suppliers for different areas. Initially, there was no standardisation of plugs and at least five different types developed, with combinations of round and square pins of various diameters and pitch circles. Almost all plugs have now been standardised, but you may occasionally run up against a round pin outlet of the old design. For domestic use, a bulky three-pin plug with square pins and containing an internal fuse is standard. If you are visiting from overseas and wish to use an electrical appliance, you will almost certainly need to convert to the British plug standard or find a suitable adapter.

Like most countries, use of computers is widespread. For those who need to use computers and have not brought your own, gaining computer access to run your own programmes should be relatively straightforward.

Geography

Britain: Geography and National Symbols

Geographical

Area	241,752 sq km
Longest River	River Severn (354 km)
Highest Mountain	Ben Nevis (1,343 m)
Bordering Countries	Ireland (length of border 360 km)
Coastline	12,429 km
Fishing Zone	200 km
Hottest Recorded Temperature	37.1°C
Lowest Recorded Temperature	-27°C

National Symbols

England	Rose
Wales	Daffodil and Leek
Scotland	Thistle

The mainland of Great Britain extends over about 9° of latitude. The southernmost point on the mainland is Lizard Point on the tip of Cornwall and the northernmost point is Dunnet Head in Caithness, Northern Scotland. Off the coast to the north of Scotland lie the Orkney and Shetland Islands and to the west, the Hebrides.

The Severn River, flowing into the Bristol Channel between South Wales and the south western counties of Devonshire and

Gloucestershire, drains the country's most important catchment basin. At 354 km, the Severn is Britain's longest river. Various other rivers, notably the Thames, the Humber, the Tyne and the Tees flow east into the North Sea.

A range of rugged hills and low mountains, the Pennines, runs along the spine of the country. The terrain of both Wales and Scotland is also mountainous. The highest peak in Britain is Ben Nevis in the highlands of Scotland, with a height of 1,343 m (4,406 ft). The highest peak in Wales is Mount Snowdon at 1,085 m (3,560 ft). Terrain in the western half of England is undulating, with much flatter country to the east of the Pennines. The fens area in eastern Britain is an extensive region of low-lying coastal land.

For a small country, Britain offers a variety of landscapes— from the pretty villages that dot most of the green and pleasant countryside to the mountainous grandeur of the Highlands and the alpine beauty of the Lake District.

Northern Ireland has its own unique brand of spectacular scenery, in particular the rugged western coast where the land ends abruptly in soaring cliffs pounded by the Atlantic Ocean.

With its range of habitats, its history and tradition, and its abundance of significant buildings and structures from many past periods of its history, the country has much to offer the tourist. Tourism is a major industry, with overseas tourists visiting Britain contributing to about 7% of the country's foreign exchange.

Getting Around Britain

Britain is served by a rail network that covers most areas of the country. Taxis are readily available for all areas of the country and work on metered fares. Taxis may either be hailed in the street or booked by phone. The country is fairly small, so domestic air services are limited. If one is travelling between city centres, point to point train travel is faster than air travel— counting trips to the airport and check in times each end of the journey—for all but extreme distances and, of course, trips between Great Britain and Northern Ireland.

Hotels

Some of the world's most famous hotels are located in Britain. (The Dorchester and the Savoy are a couple of names that spring to mind). A full range of hotels is available—from five star luxury hotels to budget price hostels. Hotels in Britain tend to be expensive. A 1998 tourism survey rated London as the world's ninth most expensive city (behind cities such as St. Petersburg, Shanghai and Tokyo.) For the tourist, bed and breakfast establishments, or B&Bs, is offered as an alternative. Here, for a fairly reasonable price, you can stay at someone's private home, often a farmhouse, almost like a member of the family.

Location

Great Britain is separated from continental Europe by the North Sea to the east and the English Channel to the south. The coastlines of south-west England and most of Scotland and Northern Ireland face the Atlantic Ocean. Between Ireland and England lies the Irish Sea.

Only 35 km wide at its narrowest point, the English Channel has been a very strategic and important stretch of sea water. For over a millennium, the "English Moat" has saved Britain from a number of European belligerents who have gathered, from time to time, on the continental side of the Channel before retiring to fight amongst themselves. The last successful European invasion of England was in 1066 A.D. by the Norman king, William the Conqueror. The most recent force to pose an invasion threat was Adolf Hitler's *Wehrmacht* of World War II.

The English Channel is also one of the world's busiest shipping lanes, serving European posts, such as Dieppe, Rotterdam and the English ports of Southampton and Portsmouth on the Britain's southern coastline.

Money

British currency is the pound sterling (£), a name derived from its origins as one pound weight of sterling silver. The symbol for the pound, based on the letter *l*, was the abbreviation of *libra*, the Latin word for pound weight.

In years past, the pound was too highly valued for day-to-day commerce. A range of smaller denomination units was spawned. Shillings at 20 to the pound and pennies at 12 to the shilling were the principal coinage. Other coins were the florin (two shillings), the half crown (two shillings and six pence), the crown (five shillings), the guinea (one pound one shilling), the half penny and the farthing (four to a penny).

In the 20th century, most of this coinage was gradually withdrawn. With the introduction of decimal currency in 1971, only two units remained—the pound and the penny (called a *new penny* at the time of decimalisation and worth 2.4 times the old penny). The conversion rate into pounds was 100 "new pennies" to the pound, as opposed to 240 "old pennies" to the pound. Gradually, the adjective *new* was dropped, so the currency is now pounds and pennies at 100 to the pound.

Public Holidays in Britain

Public holidays are a mixture of Christian holidays and bank holidays, when most banks, offices and places of interest are closed.

British public holidays include:

- New Year's Day: 1 January
- Bank Holiday in Scotland: 2 January
- Good Friday: First Friday in April (varies)
- Easter Monday (not in Scotland): Monday after Good Friday
- May Day Bank Holiday: First Monday in May
- Spring Bank Holiday: Last Monday in May
- Summer Bank Holiday: First Monday in August (Scotland), last Monday in August (outside Scotland)
- Christmas Day: 25 December
- Boxing Day: 26 December

Many people also take leave during the days between Christmas and New Year's Day.

Time and Date

In the age when Britannia ruled the waves and figuring out your longitude was the biggest problem in navigation, Britain became the leading country in developing the technology of time measurement. One method of measuring longitude was to take a very accurate clock on board your ship, then take a sunsight at noon local time and compare it to the time shown on your clock. Another was to make some very complicated astronomical observations. The Royal Navy sponsored both lines of enquiry, working closely with the Astronomer Royal at the Royal Observatory at Greenwich, just east of London. The chronometer was invented and star charts perfected. After some dispute with the French (who thought all time should start in Paris), it was internationally accepted that zero longitude passed through Greenwich Observatory and Greenwich Mean Time (GMT) became the internationally accepted basis for time.

GMT is wintertime in Britain, which is included in a single time zone. For summer time, clocks are put forward one hour and for double summer time, two hours.

Time is either quoted on 24-hour clocks or on night and day 12-hour clocks starting at midnight and noon. The European date system is based on the day/month/year standard. Thus, 6 January 1999 is written as 6/1/1999 and 1 June 1999 as 1/6/1999.

Shopping

Britain is a Mecca for shopping for some people, in particular the French. With the opening of the Channel Tunnel, some French people within easy reach of the English Channel coast find it economical to make regular shopping trips to Britain to take advantage of cheaper prices. Britain has some of the best known shops in the world, such as Harrods, that are in themselves tourist attractions. Shopping hours are becoming progressively relaxed, with 24-hour supermarket shopping not uncommon.

Directory of Important Contacts

Marketing Information

A. C. Nielsen
185 Kings Road
Reading
Berkshire RG14 EX
Tel: 0118 956 9165
Website: www.acneilson.co.uk

The Chartered Institute of Marketing
Moor Hall Cookham
Berkshire SL6 9QH
Tel: 0628 524922
Fax: 0628 531382
Website: www.cim.co.uk

Market Research Society
15 Northburgh Street
London EC1V OAH
Tel: 071 490 4911
Website:
www.marketresearch.com.uk

Office of National Statistics
Records borad-based national statistics on main economic indicators, such as GNP and inflation. Information is available by subscription at a fee through the ONS website,
www.ons.gov.uk?ons-f.htm.

Advertising Information

Advertising Standards Authority (ASA)
Brook House
2 Torrington Place
London WC1E
Tel: 0171 580 5555
Fax: 0171 631 3051
Website: www.3igroup.com

Industry Associations

Association of British Chambers of Commerce (Head office)
9 Tufton Street
London SW1P 3BQ
Tel: 0171 222 1555
Fax: 0171 799 2202
Website: www.thebiz.co.uk

Confederation of British Industry
Centrepoint
103 New Oxford Street
London WC1 AIDU
Tel: 0171 379 7400
Fax: 0171 240 0988
Website: www.cbi.org.uk

Institute of Directors
116 Pall Mall
London SW1Y 5ED
Tel: 0171 839 1233
Website: www.iod.org.uk

Government Bodies

British Standards Institute
389 Chiswick High Road
London W44AL
Tel: 01 81 9969000
Website: www.bsi.org.uk

Buckingham Palace Publicity
Whitehall
London SW1A 1AA
Tel: 0171 930 4832
Website: www.royal.gov.uk

Companies House
Crown Way Cardiff
South Glamorganshire CF43UZ
Tel: 01222 388588
Website:
www.companieshouse.gov.uk

Department of Customs and Excise
New Kings Beam House
22 UpperGround
London SE1 9PJ
Tel: 0171 6201313
Website: www.hmce.gov.uk

Department of Trade and Industry (Head office)
1 Victoria Street
London SW1 HOEX
There are various numbers for different departments:
General enquiries: 0171 255000
Business in Europe:
0117 9444888
Innovation hotline:
0171 2151217
Invest in Britain Bureau:
0171 215 2501
Single Market Complaint Unit:
0171 2156703
Website: www.dti.gov.uk

Environmental Service Division
78 Garrett Lane
London SW18 4DJ
Tel: 0181 871 6965
Website: www.ea.gov.uk

EuroInformation Centres
8 Storey's Gate
London SW1P 3AT
Tel: 071 973 1992
Website: www.cec.org.uk

Inland Revenue
Euston Tower
286 Euston Road
London NW1
Tel: 0171 667 4000
Website:
www.inlandrevenue.gov.uk

Funding Bodies

British Venture Capital Association
Essex House
12–13 Essex Street
London WC2R3AA
Tel: 0171 24038461
Website: www.bvca.co.uk

Stock Exchange of London
Threadneedle Street
London EC2
Tel: 0171 5882355
Website:
www.londonstockex.co.uk

APPENDIX C

Further Reading

Terry Tan, *Culture Shock! Britain*. Singapore: Times Editions, 1999.

Orin Hargraves, *Living and Working Abroad: London*. Singapore: Times Editions, 1999.

Peter Evans, *United Kingdom*. Parkwest Publications, 1997.
An interesting tapestry of facts and figures on the United Kingdom.

Price Waterhouse, *Doing Business in the United Kingdom*. UK: Price Waterhouse.
A frequently updated handbook on United Kingdom tax and accounting practice. While fairly formal in style, it contains most of the information you need to set up a business in Britain.

Blake's United Kingdom Book of Parliament 1998. Seven Hills Book Distributors, 1998.
A who's who of the British Parliament. An easy-to-read book on the workings of the UK political system and the connection to the EU Parliament.

Ewart James and Duncan McKinnon, *Dic Ntc's of the United Kingdom Dictionary: The Most Practical Guide to British Language and Culture*. NTC Publishing Group, 1997.
Comprehensive guide to UK culture—lavishly illustrated.

Judith E. Nichols, *Lessons from Abroad—Fresh Ideas from Fund Raising Experts in the United Kingdom*. Bonus Books, 1997.
The title is self explanatory

Gordon Wills et al., *Creating and Marketing New Products*. Grenada
Publishing Ltd, 1973.
A comprehensive volume on turning prototypes into successful
marketing ventures. Still relevant, despite its antiquity.

Notes

Chapter 1

1 The OECD includes most of the countries in Western Europe plus Japan, the United States, Canada, Australia, New Zealand, Mexico and Turkey.

2 "Euroland" is the term for a fully integrated EU coined by Wim Duisenberg, the president of the Europe European Bank.

About the Author

Qualified in engineering and economics, PETER NORTH started his career in an engineering design office before branching out to construction projects in the United Kingdom and the Middle East and mining projects in Australia, South Africa and Papua New Guinea. He later become involved in various business ventures in Australia and the United Kingdom in the construction and manufacturing industries. While in the Middle East, he lectured on business statistics and mathematics for the Golden Gate University MBA course. Later, in Thailand, he lectured on business finance for Bradford University. Other published works include *Countries of the World: Australia* (Times Editions) and *Succeed in Business: Australia* (Times Editions).

Index